WILLIAM BRADFORD

Plymouth's Faithful Pilgrim

GARY D. SCHMIDT

EERDMANS BOOKS FOR YOUNG READERS
GRAND RAPIDS, MICHIGAN / CAMBRIDGE, U.K.

Copyright © 1999 by Gary D. Schmidt
Published 1999 by Eerdmans Books for Young Readers
an imprint of Wm. B. Eerdmans Publishing Co.
255 Jefferson Ave. S.E., Grand Rapids, Michigan 49503 /
P.O. Box 163, Cambridge CB3 9PU U.K.

Printed in the United States of America

03 02 01 00 99   7 6 5 4 3 2

Library of Congress Cataloging-in-Publication Data

Schmidt, Gary D.
William Bradford: Plymouth's Faithful Pilgrim / Gary Schmidt.
p.   cm.
Includes bibliographical references and index.
ISBN 0-8028-5151-7 (cloth: alk. paper)
ISBN 0-8028-5148-7 (pbk.: alk. paper)
1. Bradford, William, 1588-1657.   2. Pilgrims (New Plymouth
Colony) — Biography.   3. Massachusetts — History —
New Plymouth, 1620-1691.   4. Plymouth (Mass.) — Biography.   I. Title.
F68.B78S36   1999
974.4′02 — dc21   97-44477
CIP

For the congregation of
Neland Avenue Christian Reformed Church,
with thanks for its answerable courage.

Contents

WILLIAM BRADFORD

Preface

November 1620. William Bradford stands at the prow of the *Mayflower*, weeks and weeks of ocean behind him, hoping the winds will pull up a blue horizon different from the gray sea that foams and parts before him. To his back is the life he might have led in England or in Holland, the life of a landowner, or a successful businessman. To his back are wealth and ease — as well as his son, judged too young to travel on the *Mayflower*. Ahead of Bradford is a strange and cold land, where there will be no one to greet him. There will be dangers and starvation and disease. There will be those determined to kill. There will be no rest, constant fear, and death for most of those on board ship.

Bradford is eager to get there.

The call comes from one of the sailors, as sharp-eyed and eager as Bradford is to make landfall after a troublesome voyage on a ship filled with sickened colonists. And within a few hours the ship, as Bradford later wrote, "fell with that land which is called Cape Cod."

Though it is land, it is not a reassuring sight. The low, windswept beach offers no shelter, and the sand slants past scrub bushes just holding their own against the wind, through knee-high beach grasses, and then into a dark wood, where anything at all might be lurking.

At this one moment, years of prayers, expectations, plans, disappointments fuse for Bradford. If others look fearfully toward the shore, he looks with eager joy. If his wife looks sadly backward, longing for her child, Bradford seems not to notice. If some look disappointed, he will ignore them. If needs must be, he will carry the colony on his own shoulders, and he will certainly be one of the very first ashore.

But here at the very wrist of Cape Cod, the *Mayflower* is exposed to all the winds swirling up from the land, as well as the ocean waves that shove them toward the shore. The sea roughens, so that the *Mayflower* is almost overtaken by "deangerous shoulds [shoals] and roring breakers." So close, the Pilgrims are forced to put out a bit from land, hoping to find a site where they can reach the shore. Yet though days, and finally weeks, will pass before the Pilgrims can step on the land that they ultimately settle, Bradford is never disappointed. He watches the shore, looking for a landfall, a place to build a colony.

He never doubts that God has brought the Pilgrims here to establish a new life, in a new world. Here the Pilgrims would build the New Jerusalem, a place where they might worship freely, where they would rule themselves according to the laws of God, where they could escape the tyranny and persecution that had followed them like shadows their whole lives. They were not coming to conquer. They were not merchants looking for wealth, like the colonists down south in Jamestown. They were coming so that they might be free to be who they were.

Bradford fairly quivered with the excitement of it. Only God's hand could have brought an orphaned shepherd boy from rural England to the outstretched arm of a new continent. That new continent might be bitterly cold and gray as a dead fire. But it was a new life that waited just across a short stretch of water.

God had given it to him.

ONE

"A Heart So to Do"

The world of Queen Elizabeth to which William Bradford was born seemed to be reeling from the energy that came down from the throne. Known for her beauty — or at least her vanity — for her red wigs and rouge, her jewels and two thousand courtly dresses, Elizabeth loomed over a court that was filled with boars' heads, spiced ale, lute music, and sonnets. It was an age when England was spreading its shoulders and sending voyagers — some called them pirates — to new discoveries in Asia and North America. If they came back with treasure looted from the Spanish, so much the better. It was the age of Shakespeare and the play, an age of elegant and formal dance, an age of vast estates and formal gardens and expensive entertainments for the queen, complete with fireworks.

Of course, not everyone was invited to sit by the queen to enjoy the fireworks. There were those who sat on the filthy city streets, those out in the countryside whose land was always subject to the whims of their lords, the ex-soldiers who wandered with no employment, the poor who were forced to steal in order to survive — and who lost their hands if caught. None of these dared approach the queen with their problems, and many found themselves thrown into prisons for no cause, places where food was rotten, bedding straw was filthy, and hallways were open sewers. The heads of those judged to be treasonous decorated the pikes of London Bridge. The splendor of Elizabeth had its dirty underside.

And truth to tell, most lived far from the court; their only contact with the queen might be a fleeting glimpse of her red wig bobbing in her coach window as the royal procession moved from manor house to manor house. Many would die in the same town — usually in the same house — in which they were born. They would do what their fathers and mothers had done before them, never anticipating that they would rise above the position of their parents, never anticipating that the seasons would bring anything beyond the expected changes. The queen was the still point around which everything else held steady.

Or at least, as steady as Elizabeth could hold it.

When Elizabeth came to the throne, she brought with her a fierce sense of her own role as queen of England and head of the Church of England (also called the Anglican Church). And England was ready to accept her as such. She established a new form of Anglican service and compelled all of her subjects to attend Sunday services in the English church. People who missed these services for more than a month, or who instead attended "any unlawful assemblies . . . or meetings under colour or pretence of any Exercise of Religion," would be imprisoned until they agreed to conform. If after three months they still refused to conform, they would be exiled. If they returned to England, they would be executed.

It was the most severe act of Elizabeth's reign, and it posed the

Austerfield, William Bradford's birthplace

most severe questions for any person whose beliefs differed even slightly from those of the Church of England. Elizabeth, like her father Henry VIII, was assuming the headship of a church. But could a sovereign demand that everyone worship in precisely the same way? Was it permissible for someone to read the Scriptures and come to conclusions that might be different from the established church? And if one were to come up with ideas different from those held by the queen's church, should such a person feel compelled to attend the state church still? Could one leave and set up a church of one's own? Could a group of people have the right to establish their own church, with a pastor of their own choice?

These were dangerous questions to ask a sovereign. To ask them meant that it would be possible to disagree with the queen's rulings, and this the queen would never permit.

But in the little hamlet of Austerfield, one hundred and fifty miles from London, a group of people were asking just those sorts of questions. No one in Austerfield had ever been to the great city of London; few had even left Yorkshire to travel on the Great North Road, which was really just a cart path, not infrequently visited by highwaymen. The surrounding countryside was mostly marsh, moors, and bogs. Where the ground was higher, there were grazing pastures. Where the ground had not been cleared, there were ancient forests. Where the eye could travel past the woods, it found rolling hills that protected the fields all the way down to the Idle. Perhaps Queen Elizabeth had never even heard of it.

But here, William Bradford's family had lived for generations, not far from the stone church where the Anglican services were read. Though the family would have seemed inconsequential to the court of London, in Austerfield the Bradfords were prominent. For four generations they had been buying land and houses in several different towns. Bradford's grandfather, also named William, bought land in Austerfield, in Bawtry to the south, and in Mission, even farther to the south and over the Nottinghamshire border. The wills of these Bradfords suggest that they were, if not wealthy, not poor. In a time when most people used wooden spoons, theirs were silver. They lay in comfort on feather beds, not straw mattresses, and they had flocks of lambs.

William, in fact, was born during lambing season, when most of the family was out in the fields and the pens, tending the sheep. He was baptized in the parish church on March 29, 1590, beginning his life in accord with the religious traditions that his queen so approved. He was the heir to all the family lands, as well as the flocks of lambs being born around him. But in this season, he had to share the family's attention with the demands of the farm: the plowing and manuring, the raking and sowing in May, the sheepshearing in

Harvest season, part of farm life in Austerfield

June, the haying in July to store up the winter's feed, the harvest in August, the threshing in September, and the cider-making and slaughtering in late fall. From his earliest days he fell into the rhythms of the farm life, rhythms which would later prove valuable in his life in Plymouth Colony.

During the first seven years of his life, Bradford was a part of all the daily chores that made a productive farm. He watched his mother in the dairy, tending the milkers. He saw her brew the beer in the brewhouse. In the hall, he saw her cook in the great fireplace, roasting and broiling and baking meat and vegetables and bread to accompany the butter and cheese from the dairy. Bradford himself helped to card and spin the sheep wool, and learned how to tend the sheep. He also learned how to handle the cattle, driving them to their fields, hitching them to their carts, and holding the plow behind them.

It seems as if it might have been a quiet life filled with delights and work and the pleasure that work gives. But it was not. In Elizabeth's England death came quickly and often to a household, and though William and his sister Alice escaped, his sister Margaret and his parents did not. He was only sixteen months old when William Bradfourth, his father, was buried by the Austerfield church. He had been married only seven years; his son would have no memories of him at all. He left his wife, Alice Hanson, with fine property and goods, and Alice herself came from a rather wealthy family of shopkeepers and farmers. But she had three children and a farm to cultivate, and the tasks must have seemed almost unbearable. So, when William was four years old, she married again, leading to yet another separation: young William was sent to live with his grandfather.

Bradford would never have a close-knit family. Two years after leaving his mother, William found his grandfather dead. He returned to Austerfield to live with his mother and stepfather, but had been there only one year when, in 1597, his mother died; at seven years old, William Bradford was an orphan. He did not stay with his stepfather, but went to live instead with two uncles, Robert and Thomas. It was clear that he could be useful to them, if yet another mouth to feed. They set him "unto the affairs of husbandry," the task Bradfords had been doing for generations.

The rapid changes and losses had their effects, however: a "soon and long sickness" afflicted him. Though it was painful, Bradford came to see his illness as a blessing, since he was able to turn to reading instead of shepherding. At first his uncles saw the sickness in a different light: there was less that Bradford could do to contribute to the life of the farm. But if young William were to learn to write, he could be a help. In an age when very few men and fewer women could write at all — in fact, when few could even sign their names — the ability to write gave certain advantages to a family such as the Bradfords. William would be able to draft deeds, to keep accounts, and to conduct the family business.

There was no school in Austerfield, so Bradford probably received his education from a local minister, perhaps the Reverend Silvester of Alkley, who had a library of both English and Latin books. Here he would have read books of theology — all approved by Elizabeth's church. He would have read Desiderius Erasmus's satirical work *The Praise of Folly,* which would have opened up Europe to a boy who had never ventured beyond his Yorkshire hills. He would have read John Foxe's *Book of Martyrs,* one of the most popular books of the age which, with gory and bloody details, told of the martyrdoms of Christians under Bloody Mary, Queen Elizabeth's sister. And he would have read the Bible — a feat that few in England could have achieved and which many in the clergy would have feared. The Bible, the clergy argued, was for churchmen to interpret, not for any "Jack & Tom, & Will & Dick" to be reading. But by age twelve, Bradford was deeply immersed in the Scriptures. Left frail and weak by his sickness, he found studies more to his liking than farming.

But this reading had unexpected consequences. Though he had attended the Austerfield church with his uncles, his reading in the Bible made him wonder if Queen Elizabeth's church was the only right and true way. Just a few miles down the Great North Road, in Babworth, a Richard Clyfton was preaching that the English church needed to be reformed. Sometime after his twelfth year, Bradford met a boy about his own age who invited him to go to the church at

7

The church at Austerfield

Babworth to hear Clyfton. William walked the eight miles to hear a preacher whom, in later years, he called "a grave and fatherly old man." Perhaps it was that "fatherly" quality that attracted Bradford; but perhaps he was attracted because Clyfton was preaching ideas that had come to him also.

His uncles did not approve, however; they were appalled. Clyfton, they argued, was one of the "fantastical schismatics" who so worried the Crown. To attend his church was a particularly dangerous thing for a member of one of the more important families in the area; he would almost certainly be noticed, and he would bring disgrace upon the family — if not worse. His uncles forbade

his attendance at Babworth. They told him that if he would not return to Saint Helen's Church, where his family had worshiped for
so long, he would lose his reputation, his soul, and all of the family
lands.

All of these threats must have struck young Bradford keenly. It
was extraordinary for a boy just into his teens to set himself against
his family, his church, his sovereign. He was bringing himself and
his family into disrepute and threatening the inheritance for which
his grandfather and great-grandfather had worked so hard. Nevertheless, he began to walk sixteen miles each Sunday to attend the
Babworth church.

If his uncles admired the strength of Bradford's faith, they did
not show it; perhaps they saw it as mere stubbornness. The friend
who first introduced Bradford to Clyfton abandoned him, perhaps
under similar threats from his family. Neighbors laughed at his asso-
ciation with the Babworth church. But neither "the wrath of his
uncles, nor the scoff of his neighbors . . . diverted him from his
pious inclinations." In fact, Bradford told his uncles, if he was to suffer disaster because of his new beliefs, then he would be suffering
"for a good Cause." They should neither be angry with him nor feel
sorry for him, he insisted, because God had called him to follow in
this way, and "hath given me a heart so to do."

It is hard to imagine that Bradford would have withstood all of
the pressures toward conformity that were every day increasing had
he not found someone to give him support. He did. Halfway between Austerfield and Babworth was Scrooby Manor, the dwelling
of William Brewster. Brewster was thirty-seven when he first met
the adolescent Bradford, but he quickly became a friend, a teacher,
and, in many ways, a father to Bradford. They had both been asking
the same kinds of questions. Brewster was able to lend books to
Bradford, and to encourage him in the choices he had made. And he

William Brewster

stood against Bradford's uncles; as one living in the bishop's palace, Brewster had a kind of prestige that would impress them.

As they walked together across the fields to Babworth, Brewster told his young friend of what was happening in Britain, particularly in her churches. Brewster would have had much to say, for he had seen more of the world than anyone living at Austerfield. Educated at Cambridge University, he had begun what looked to be a brilliant political career, traveling to Holland with Sir William Davison, the British ambassador, where he witnessed firsthand a tiny nation struggling against the huge power of Spain for its national and religious freedom. When the ambassador negotiated a loan from the English to the Dutch, the Dutch, as security, gave the ambassador three keys to their fortifica-

Scrooby Manor, William Brewster's home

tions; Brewster was entrusted with these, and he slept with them under his pillow. When they left Holland, the ambassador was presented with a gold chain as a memorial; he directed Brewster to wear this when they were presented at the court of Elizabeth herself.

But if Brewster had seen the glittering side of the court, he also had seen its ugliness. Two years after his return, Elizabeth signed the death warrant for her half sister, Mary Queen of Scots. When she saw that the execution was unpopular, she looked for someone else to blame and settled upon her faithful servant, Ambassador Davison. She had him thrown into the Tower of London for two years and all of his lands and wealth confiscated. Several of the nobles close to Elizabeth pleaded his case, but she would not listen. Brewster, despite the danger, remained faithful to Davison and finally, rejecting the court as well as the patronage of Davison's friends, returned to his family home at Scrooby.

Brewster lived in some comfort, in a government post with an assured salary. He could have lived a quiet, reposed life, but he did not. Hoping that he would remain unnoticed, Brewster began to encourage the Anglican worshippers in his area to search for educated, godly pastors, especially since many of the churches had had their pastors removed by Elizabeth. He hoped that they would choose "Puritan" pastors, men who believed that the Church of England should be reformed. He encouraged congregations to rebuild their churches, many of which were decaying, and he urged people to attend services and care for the poor in the community, often sending money himself as an encouragement.

When Queen Elizabeth died in 1603 and James I became king, Brewster, along with the Puritans, believed that perhaps now there would be change in England, and people would be granted the liberty of their consciences.

But Brewster was to be disappointed. When the Puritans approached James to ask for reform, he was enraged. "I will none of that!" he thundered; a church in which its members made their own choices about how they were to be governed "as well agreeth with a Monarchy as God and the Devil. Then Jack & Tom, & Will and Dick, shall meete and at their pleasure censure me, and my Council, and all our proceedings." James would not be censured. He swore that he would put down anyone who challenged his authority as head of the church. "I will make them conform, or I will harry them out of the land."

In fact, this last was a lie. He would not harry them out of the land — he would imprison them, as William Bradford and his friends would soon discover, to their sorrow.

By 1606, when Bradford was sixteen, many of the Puritan min-

King James I

isters that Brewster had encouraged to come to the destitute churches around Scrooby were driven from their pulpits, and all of Brewster's work was undone. Now, with James I asserting all of the prerogatives that Elizabeth had asserted, it became a dangerous thing to even speak of reforming the established church. At Babworth, Richard Clyfton chose to resign. At Scrooby, Bradford and Brewster realized that their world was now more threatening.

Perhaps Bradford's uncles were pleased with Clyfton's resignation, but if so, they did not anticipate what would be, for them, a much worse situation. Twelve miles away from Austerfield, in

Gainsborough, a church similar to the one at Babworth had formed. Upon Clyfton's resignation, Bradford turned his feet to the east, crossing the River Trent to reach this congregation. He was a member when, in 1606, under the new pastor John Smyth, the church decided that reform of the English church was impossible. It would become Separatist, a church that would try to sever all connections with the Church of England.

This was a dangerous decision, but there seems to have been no hesitation on the part of Brewster or his young friend Bradford. Now, since the distance from Austerfield and Babworth to Gainsborough was so great, the congregation split into two, the smaller portion of about forty or fifty people meeting instead at Austerfield. They assembled in secret at Scrooby Manor, Brewster's residence, hoping they would not be noticed, where Brewster served them food and drink "with great love . . . making provision for them to his great charge." They asked Richard Clyfton to be the minister for the Scrooby group, and he accepted — not an easy choice for a minister who had been in the Anglican Church his entire life.

Bradford had taken the next step upon a very dangerous pilgrimage. His uncles were now even more determined to put an end to his stubbornness. They told him that he was disgracing his family, that he was endangering himself. Other family members added their voices, all trying to bring Bradford's feet back to the path that they had trod for so long. But when one of his uncles suddenly died, Bradford, and apparently his family, saw this as a sign. From that time on, there is no record of attempts on the part of his family to bring him out of the Separatist church.

However, it is unlikely that any such attempts would have succeeded; Bradford had found a new purpose and a new mentor, quite different from uncles eager to have him tending flocks.

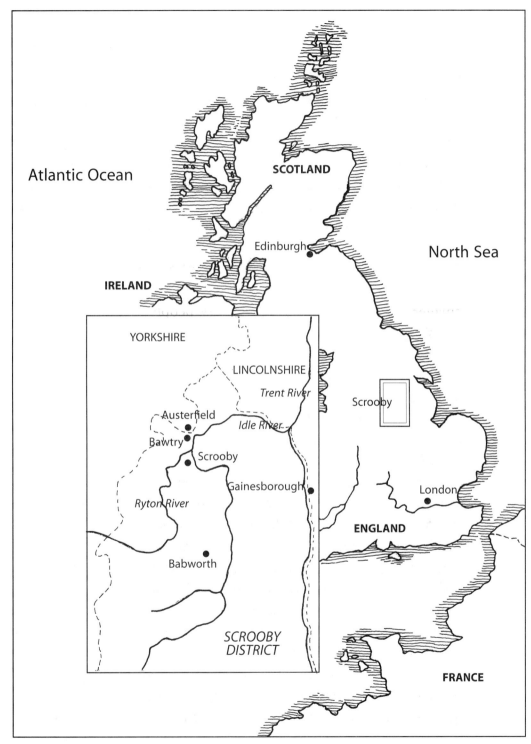

Map of England highlighting the Scrooby/Austerfield area

Brewster and Bradford grew quite close, and the virtues that Bradford saw in Brewster suggest what he valued in a friend. Brewster, wrote Bradford,

> was wise and discreete and well spoken, having a grave and deliberate utterance, of a very cheerful spirit, very sociable & pleasante amongst his friends, of an humble and modest mind, of peaceable disposition, undervaluing himself & his owne abilities, and some time overvaluing others: inoffensive and innocent in his life & conversation, which gained him the love of those without, as well as those within. . . . He was tenderhearted, and compassionate to such as were in misery. . . . In teaching, he was very moving & stirring of affections, also very plaine & distincte in what he taught.

The gentle spirit, the humility, the wisdom — all of these qualities would mark Bradford's time as governor later in his life. Though these qualities may have been innate in him, perhaps, too, they were nurtured by the example of his good friend.

The Scrooby group continued in its congregational life through the spring and summer of 1607, but not without fear. As Bradford was studying Latin under the direction of Brewster, he was also hearing of other Separatists who were judged to be traitors and executed. Bradford wrote that they had "shook off this yoke of antichristian bondage, and as the Lords free people, joined themselves (by covenant of the Lord) into a church estate, in the fellowship of the gospel, to walke in all his wayes, made known, or to be made known unto them, according to their best endeavours, whatsoever it should cost them, the Lord assisting them." As they met secretly, they knew it would cost much; when the Brewsters had a second daughter, they named her, appropriately, Fear.

By the fall of 1607, the Separatists began to sense the costs. In

London, Separatists were thrown in prison by the droves. Anglican bishops saw them as a threat to their own authority, and so, simply by accusing people of being Separatists — with no evidence — the bishops could have them arrested and put in prison. There they lay for months and even years without trial, "perishing," as Bradford wrote, "by cold, hunger, or noisomeness of the prison."

In his *First Dialogue*, written many years later, Bradford wrote of sixty accused of being Separatists as "being made close prisoners, allowing them neither meat, drink, fire nor lodging, nor suffering any whose hearts the Lord would stir up for their relief, to have any access unto them; so as they complain that no felons, traitors, or murderers in the land were thus dealt with." Bradford was right here; no felons, traitors, or murderers posed the kind of basic threat to the sovereign and the church that these Separatists caused.

In a small village like Austerfield, with only two hundred people, the arrival each Sunday of forty or fifty people could scarcely have gone unnoticed, especially when they walked into the home of a town official like Brewster. So in the fall of 1607, perhaps to avoid gossip, Brewster resigned from his post. But it was not enough. At the end of the year, five members of the Scrooby congregation were summoned before the Ecclesiastical Commissioners of the province of York. One of these five was William Brewster.

He and the others were judged to be "disobedient in matters of religion" and fined; they were fortunate to escape without imprisonment. Others of the congregation were jailed, however, such as the "very daingerous" Gervase Neville, charged with making "contemptuous & scandalous" speeches and meeting secretly to hold illegal church services. Bradford wrote of the tense and dangerous atmosphere: some members "were taken & clapt up in prison; others had their houses besett & watched night and day, & hardly escaped their hands; and the most were faine to fly & leave their houses & habita-

17

tions, and the means of their livelehood." Their former troubles, suggested Bradford, "were but as flea-bitings in comparison of these which now came upon them."

The "peaceable condition" in which they had lived had drawn to a close. Perhaps Bradford's position as the heir of two of Austerfield's most important families had protected him, but there could be no assurance that this would last; neighbors "scoffed and scorned them," and Bradford must have known that the day would come when he too would be called before the Ecclesiastical Commissioners. Clyfton and his congregation began to think seriously of a plan that they had thought of before. It was a plan that would mean religious freedom. It was a plan that would bring an end to the persecution in England. And it was a plan that would mean exile.

The predictions of Bradford's uncles were coming true, and Bradford rushed forward to meet them.

TWO

"An Adventure Almost Desperate"

For generations the families of Austerfield, Gainsborough, and Babworth had held to the land. It had been their income, their heritage, their wealth, their pride. They had worked the fields in all seasons; walked across the roads of these towns to births, marriages, and burials; played and sweated in — and loved — fields as familiar to them as their own breath. And now the Separatists that gathered at William Brewster's house began to think of leaving those fields forever and fleeing to the Netherlands. There they would no longer have to meet secretly; there they would worship exactly as they felt God called upon them to worship.

But they would lose their land, their country, their way of life, their families and friends, their language itself. They were farmers, not merchants or tradesmen; the skills they had learned on the farm would be of no use in Amsterdam. Bradford wrote that "to goe into a countrie they knew not (but by hearsay), where they must learne a new language, and get their livings they knew not how, it being a dear place, & subjecte to the miseries of war, it was by many thought an adventure almost desperate, a case intolerable, & a miserie worse then death."

But for William Bradford and the other Separatists at Scrooby, there really was no choice. If they did not go, their congregation would be destroyed. As for their fears, "they rested on [God's] providence, & knew whom they had believed." Quietly, Clyfton and many of the families of the church at Scrooby converted their leases into cash and sold their landholdings. Gathering together the money, the group secretly contracted with a ship to take them to Holland. Late in 1607, the group began to walk toward Boston on the Wash, sixty miles to the southeast, carrying with them whatever goods they wished to bring with them into exile. They hoped they would not attract any attention.

They had good reason to be afraid. Despite James's threat to "harry them out of the land," he preferred to imprison and persecute his subjects rather than let them escape. The ship captain who would transport the Scrooby congregation knew this; undoubtedly much of the money that came from the sale of the Scrooby property went to the captain as a bribe.

The Separatists arranged for a meeting, probably at night, when the captain would put in "at a conveniente place"; Bradford, writing about this escape decades after the event, never revealed where this meeting was to take place. But on the night he was to meet them, the captain did not appear. The Separatists waited eagerly, in local inns, knowing that the presence of this large a group of people would not escape the attention of those who lived in Boston. Finally, after several days, the ship did put in one night and the Separatists all climbed aboard with what goods they had. Bradford, seventeen years old, was leaving his entire family behind him.

But the imprisonment and the disgrace that his uncles had predicted were about to fall upon him. The reasons for the captain's tardiness became apparent, as Bradford remembered bitterly. "But when he had them & their goods aboard, he betrayed them, having before hand ploted with the searchers & other officers so to do; who tooke them, and put them into open boats, & there rifled & ransaked them, searching them to their shirts for money, yea even the women further than became modestie." All was lost: the money for the ship, the bribe, the small properties by which they would remember their former homes, their books — everything.

The group was brought back into Boston, closely guarded by constables, where they were made "a spectackle & wonder to the multitude, which came flocking on all sides to behold them." They were dragged before the magistrates of the town and imprisoned; messengers hurried to London to inform King James's court of the attempted escape. But the court was not much interested in a small band of farmers from way out in Austerfield trying to leave the country; they posed little danger.

So the Separatists were kept in prison for a month. Those who were seen as the leaders were kept on for trial; these included William Brewster; Clyfton; Clyfton's assistant, John Robinson; and four others. The rest were sent back to their homes, though for many those homes were gone, sold off to pay for the flight to the Netherlands. Bradford was among this group and must have returned to his uncle's home, to a reception that is not difficult to imagine. Brewster, Clyfton, and the others were eventually released as being too unimportant for further trial. Of all, Brewster suffered the most, as he lost virtually all of his property. He would live in poverty for some years as a result of this failed escape.

A hard winter descended upon England, made harder for the Separatists by their destitute situations. A number of the Scrooby congregation abandoned the idea of flight to the Netherlands, but

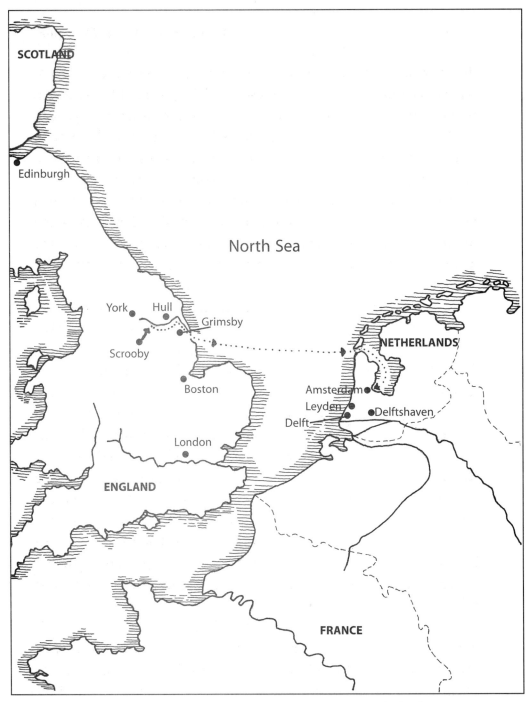

The route the Separatists took from England to the Netherlands

the majority held firm, and with the coming of spring they began to hope once more that they could escape. Selling what little remained of their household goods, they made arrangements for passage with a Dutch captain who had a ship on the North Sea coast, "hoping to find more faithfulness in him, than in the former of their own nation. He bade them not fear, for he would do well enough."

The Dutch captain agreed to meet them on the coast between Hull and Great Grimsby, at the lonely Grimsby Common at the mouth of the Humber River, where it would be easy to transport the people and their goods across to the ship. All seemed secure. The Separatists even decided to split up as a group so that they would not attract attention. The men set out across country to the east, walking the forty miles to the appointed spot. The women and children, accompanied by the families' cargo, sailed in a small bark down "Scrooby Water," later known as the Ryton River, into the Idle, then into the Trent, and finally into the Humber. It was hoped that all this could be done without attracting any attention at all.

But when the women and children arrived at the rendezvous, they found that they had made better speed than the men and would have to sit a full day. Because of seasickness on board, the women persuaded the boatmen to take them into a small, still creek into which the sea ran; there they would wait out the night. But when the men arrived in the morning, the tide had turned and run low, so that the bark was aground, with swamps and unknown channels lying between it and the shore. It would not be able to be moved until noon.

With the Separatist men on the shore, unable to reach their wives and families in the bark, the Dutch captain grew uneasy; he knew the dangers of this "adventure almost desperate." Quickly the captain sent out the ship's single boat to at least begin to load his ship; the boat brought half of the men aboard. But just as the boat set out to bring back the other half, the captain saw what he had feared all along: a crowd rushing toward the beach, "both horse & foote, with . . . guns, & other weapons, for the countrie was raised to take them."

The captain, seeing his livelihood threatened, panicked. With a fair wind behind him, he "weighed Anchor, hoisted sails, and away." He abandoned the remaining half of the men, as well as the women and children. Sailing away, the men on board watched as the crowd gathered on the beach and threatened their families, knowing there was nothing they could do to help them; the captain would not turn around. "It drew tears from their eyes, and anything they would have given to have been a shore againe; but all in vaine, ther was no remedy, they must thus sadly part."

The men who remained on Grimsby Common had little time to act. They knew they would be imprisoned, and would probably never again have a chance to escape. So they decided to flee, leaving the women and children stranded in the bark. It was hoped, and correctly so, that they would not be prosecuted, as they were simply following their husbands. Nevertheless, Bradford and Brewster remained behind "to be assistante unto the women."

The crowd, armed with pikes and guns, found an unresisting group of people. They arrested the two men and waited until the tide turned to arrest the women and children, probably confiscating the group's belongings in the meantime. "But pitifull it was to see the heavie case of these poor women in this distress; what weeping & crying on every side, some for their husbands, that were caried away in the ship . . . ; others not knowing what should become of them, & their little ones; others againe melted in teares, seeing their poore litle ones hanging aboute them, crying for feare, and quaking with cold." The scene remained stark and dramatic in Bradford's mind for the rest of his life.

They were dragged from one magistrate to another, but not a one knew what to do with them. In exasperation, they were ordered to return to their homes once more, and so they did, after having been "turmoyled a good while." Yet again, however, they had no homes to return to, and even less property than before.

They might have been even more turmoiled had they known what was happening on board the Dutch ship. Even as Bradford and Brewster stoutly watched the crowd descend upon them, the Dutch ship was sailing away from the Humber and to sea. Though this voyage normally took only a day or two, they would be at sea for fourteen days, during seven of which "they neither saw sun, moone, nor stars, & were driven near the coast of Norway; the mariners themselves often despairing of life; and once with shrieks & cries gave over all, as if the ship had been foundered in the sea, & they sinking without recoverie."

After persecution at home, imprisonment, failed attempts at escape from England, and the loss of their families, this storm at sea must have seemed one more "adventure almost desperate." At one point a savage wave struck the ship and laid it over on its beam-ends, so that the sailors cried out that they were sinking. For a group of farmers from the interior of England, this must have seemed like the end. And yet, when the ship righted itself and floated again, the Separatists saw in this evidence of God's mercy and mastery over all things; as the sailors returned to their tasks, leaving their panic behind, the Separatists saw God's hand in the return of their courage. They prayed continually, banded together on the deck, and were not distracted even "when the water ran into their mouthes & ears; and the mariners cried out."

And so, the first of the group of Separatists began their pilgrimage and landed in the city of Amsterdam. They had escaped. They had lost all their property and livelihoods. They had lost their native country, and even their families. Since all their cargo had been on the bark with the women, they had nothing more than the clothes on their backs and whatever coins they might have had in their pockets. But they had arrived in the Netherlands.

William Bradford, however, had still not escaped.

Now began something extraordinary. After the group's first attempted escape, in 1607, the King's Privy Council had dismissed the case of the Scrooby congregation as hardly worth noticing. But now, less than a year later, their case became more and more public, and their cause became famous. Stories were passed around of how well these people had borne up under persecution, so that others began to look into their principles of worship and were moved to join them. While some of the original Scrooby group abandoned their cause, tired of the difficulties that they had endured — Bradford writes that this "was no marvell" — yet newcomers "came on with fresh courage, & greatly animated others."

Perhaps it was for this reason that the authorities stopped trying to prevent their escape; they feared that the movement would spread. Or perhaps it was simply because "they were glad to be ridd of them in the end upon any termes; for all were wearied & tired with them." Or perhaps, as Bradford suggests, the pilgrimage was inevitable, for "in the end necessitie forste a way for them."

In any case, the Separatists took a new strategy: instead of escaping as a large crowd, they came over little by little, arriving in different ports at different times, "and mette together againe according to their desires, with no small rejoycing." They gathered together in Amsterdam, William Brewster, Richard Clyfton, and John Robinson remaining until the very end to ensure that all who wished to escape could begin their pilgrimage. It was a dangerous move for these three, especially for Brewster, since he was under orders in 1608 to appear before the archbishop of York.

For Bradford, there was one more indignity to be endured, one more instance of his uncles' prophecy coming true. Arriving in the port of Middleburg in the Netherlands, he was arrested as a fugitive from English justice, this on the accusation of a fellow passenger. It was a false report and he was soon cleared, but Bradford must have heaved a sigh at the trials that he and the others had undergone.

He, too, now journeyed to Amsterdam, and when Richard Clyfton and his family finally arrived in August of 1608, the last of the Scrooby congregation to come, Bradford would have gathered with the rest on the banks of the Zuyder Zee to sing praises to God. For Clyfton, now an old man by the standards of the times at fifty-six, this was an ending. To Bradford, at eighteen, it was a beginning.

There were only three full households from the Scrooby congregation that settled in Amsterdam whose names are known. Bradford was part of the Brewster household, which included William, his wife, and their three children. The Robinson household also had three children, and the Clyftons had three sons. These sixteen souls may have constituted the core group of the Scrooby congregation that, after so many setbacks, had retained the vision that inspired both Brewster and Bradford, and would eventually lead that household to the New World.

But that came later. In the meantime, Amsterdam must have seemed new enough to Bradford. Here was the place that he had worked so hard to reach, but everything in it was so strange to him. From the tiny village of Austerfield, he had arrived in a great city of 240,000 people. It was a city of narrow lanes, oddly built houses, and interlocking canals. The native language seemed to the Separatists to be "uncouth." The war between Holland and Spain had so

One of Amsterdam's
narrow lanes

wearied both countries that they had paused for a decade of peace, but warships still lay at anchor in the ports, armies still marched by the borders, and cities still garrisoned themselves against a siege. The wheels that moved Amsterdam were the wheels of commerce, and it was commerce on a worldwide scale, not the commerce of bartering and exchanging that marked the rural communities of Yorkshire.

Of all these strange and new parts of life that Bradford and the other Separatists met in Amsterdam, this last was the most frightening. Having lost everything in the attempts to come over, they were

A canal in Amsterdam

hardly prepared to start a whole new life. To simply survive, they were forced to take the easiest, most unskilled positions they could find; these were, unfortunately, also the lowest paid positions. They worked in the textile trade, or with metal or leather. Bradford saw "the grimme & grisly face of povertie coming upon them like an armed man." There were no kitchen gardens to turn to here; the threat of starvation was very real. Nevertheless, as the Separatists had during the seven-day storm, as they had in all their difficulties, they turned to God. Against poverty, the Separatists brought "faith & patience."

But not all was "grimme & grisly" in Amsterdam. In fighting against Spain, the Dutch had been fighting against a country that was determined to force them to worship as Catholics. Because the war had been carried out in the name of the church, the Dutch were eager to avoid the kind of religious hatred that would lead to similar conflicts. Thirty years before the Separatists came to Amsterdam, the Dutch had declared that no "inquiries should be made into any man's belief or conscience, or that any injury or hindrance should be offered to any man on account of his religion." With this spirit guiding the country — an extraordinary one for its time — the Separatists realized that here they would be free to worship precisely as they pleased, free from the entanglements of the Anglican Church.

Bradford began to worship in a meetinghouse on what would be called Brownists Alley, following the "Holy Discipline of Christ." For the Sabbath, this discipline was severe indeed. Bradford would arrive at the meetinghouse by eight in the morning, and the congregation would stand for an hour during the opening prayer. There was no kneeling, neither as relief nor as a sign of penitence, since it recalled too much the Church of England. The psalm that followed the opening prayer was sung unaccompanied by any instrument, since an organ was "the Divill's bag-pipes" and again recalled the Church of England. The psalm was followed by a sermon that lasted for several hours, and was followed by another psalm, and then communion. A collection was taken, the benediction spoken, and the congregation dismissed for its noon lunch.

Bradford returned not long after lunch for the second service, which again opened with a long prayer. There was no music in this service, and only a short sermon, though this too would have gone on for quite some time. It was followed by something that the Church of England, with its sense of hierarchy, could never have imagined: a general discussion. During this time, called "prophecying," a few learned men of the congregation discussed a text from the Scriptures, the minister summing up at the end to avoid all confusion and dissension.

Back in England, the Separatists were mocked for their long sermons, for their "prophecying," for their lengthy prayers. Bishops of the Church of England suggested that the Separatists had been "Amsterdamnified by brainlesse opinions" and that "a Pope and a Bishop were all one with them." To the first, the Separatists may not have given answer. To the second, they would have agreed. A pope and a bishop were all one to them. This sense of democracy that they practiced in the Amsterdam church, this sense that all Christians could have ideas that should be discussed, that bishops and archbishops were not the only authorities — these ideas were to carry over into the Plymouth Colony and influence the course of a nation.

They were also mocked for arguing about tiny points of doctrine, since they were merely "rude, mechanick fellowes." That mockery was perhaps not far off the mark. There were heated arguments with other Separatist congregations who had escaped to the Netherlands earlier, flaring into personal quarrels. Some of these were aired publicly and shocked even the tolerant citizens of Amsterdam. So the Scrooby group decided it was time for them to leave in order to find the harmony they so eagerly sought.

They had been in Amsterdam only nine months when they decided to move twenty-two miles to the southwest, to the city of Leyden.

Bradford, always discerning and able to think practically, knew there would be heavy costs to such a move; the Scrooby congregation was only just settling in and finding ways to earn an income. If they left now, all of that would be lost; as Bradford wrote, it would be "much to the prejudice of their outward estats." Nevertheless, it was decided to move. But Pastor Clyfton had come to the end of his service; he would remain in Amsterdam and send instead his assistant, John Robinson, to find a place for the congregation. So Robinson asked the burgomeisters (the town officials) of Leyden for per-

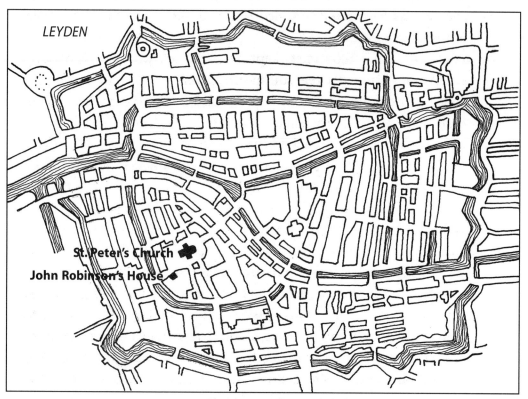

An overview of Leyden

mission to settle with about one hundred persons. He asked that the group be allowed to carry on its trade "without being a burden in the least to anyone." The burgomeisters, who had probably heard about the quarrels in Amsterdam, agreed with a subtle warning: they would be pleased to welcome all "honest" persons who would behave themselves.

And so the Separatists kept on with their pilgrimage, moving twenty-two miles to the southwest to one of the most beautiful cities in the world, a city of "sweete situation" on the Rhine River, built upon some thirty islands that were linked by 145 bridges.

As Bradford approached the city from the water, he must have looked with some longing at some of the world's richest meadows, remembering his own youth and how it was now behind him. This city, less than half the size of Amsterdam, was a place of industry rather than commerce; it was known as a city of weavers. It was to this trade that the Separatists now turned.

William Brewster's son became a ribbon weaver; others became wool carders or combers, hatters, weavers of baize and serge, and twine spinners. Some took positions not directly associated with weaving: these became masons, carpenters, brewers, bakers, cabinet-makers, tailors, and some, like John Carver, merchants, depending upon their skills. Bradford apprenticed himself to a baize or corduroy maker so that he might learn the trade from a master. Eventually Bradford and some of the other Separatists were to do so well that they set up their own manufactures, but now, in the summer of 1609, life was hard yet again as the group began to learn their trades from the very lowest positions.

For Bradford, the move to Leyden had led to serious losses. Clyfton was now gone, as was the trade in French silk that Bradford had been learning back in Amsterdam. The move had also brought the group once again to the attention of King James back in En-

John Robinson's house in Leyden was used for Sunday services.

gland, who had his ambassador to Leyden protest to the burgomeisters, claiming that the Separatists were merely English fugitives. The burgomeisters brushed aside the protest, saying they would admit any person of any religious faith.

The Separatists led a quiet life, trying, as they had promised the burgomeisters, not to be a burden to anyone. For two years they struggled, finding housing as best they could. The group settled around one of the city's old Catholic cathedrals, the Pieterskerk, or Saint Peter's Church, in a poor and crowded area cut through and

The Leyden garden around which the Pilgrims lived.
The roof of St. Peter's Church is visible in the background.

through by winding lanes and alleys. Bradford lived still with the Brewsters in their home in the Stincksteeg, or Stink Alley. It was a dank, dark alley at that time, only five feet wide and filled with infection and fumes. While they lived there, the Brewsters lost a child to sickness, and they were not the only Separatist family to suffer this sadness — a sign of their poverty.

In 1611, William Bradford was twenty-one and came of age. The property that his father had left him was now legally his, but

England was closed to him. He sold the house, the cottage, the gardens and orchards that had been his inheritance, and set himself up as a weaver.

In May of that year, perhaps using some of Bradford's newly claimed money, the Separatists bought a large old house in Klocksteeg named Groenepoort, or Green Gate; it faced the south transept of the Pieterskerk. For the two years prior to that, they probably met in each other's homes for Sunday services, but now they had a meetinghouse — the first one uniquely their own. They installed John Robinson as their minister, and he and his wife, their three children, and their maid all moved in. In the garden behind the house, opening onto the Donckeregrafte, they built twenty-one tiny houses for the poorer members of the congregation. This was relative, however, for in fact they were all poor, and poorer now with the purchase of the meetinghouse, for in each of the next three years they would have to pay a five-hundred-guilder mortgage.

Nevertheless, the Separatists had settled; they began a life "in a comfortable condition, enjoying much sweete & delightful societie & spirituall comforte together in the wayes of God, under the able ministrie and prudent governmente of Mr. John Robinson & Mr. William Brewster. . . . So . . . they grew in knowledge & other gifts & graces of the spirit of God, & lived together in peace, & love, and holiness." It must have seemed to Bradford that the Separatists had finally found what they had been looking for.

THREE

"Resolved to Proseede"

On March 30, 1612, William Bradford became a citizen of Leyden and a member of one of the Leyden guilds — the only way he could hope to prosper in his trade. He was twenty-two years old and fluent in Dutch, and had cut his last ties with England. He had used part of his money from the sale of his English land to buy a small house on the Achtergracht, or Back Canal, close to the University of Leyden. He had also purchased a loom in order to start his own business out of his house. And it was his house. For the first time in his life, he was living in a home that he owned.

At the end of this year, he returned to Amsterdam briefly to marry Dorothy May, or Dority as she signed her name. (She was the daughter of another Separatist family whom he had thought too young to marry when he first came to Amsterdam.) There was no religious service, as the Separatists could find no example of such a thing in the Scriptures. After a civil service, they returned to the

Achtergracht and began their life together among this group of English emigrants.

It was a time of peace, and yet change, for the Separatists. Some of the Scrooby congregation had remained behind in Amsterdam with Clyfton, but they were replaced by other refugees from James's intolerance who now joined Robinson's congregation. In the years at Leyden, forty-six of the Separatists were married, so that soon the families were thickly interrelated. Thirty-three men became Dutch citizens in order to join the guilds; these families were prospering. Children were coming, including Bradford's own new son, John, born in 1614 and probably named after the pastor. Leyden had indeed been free in its acceptance of their style of worship, and the entire congregation was now meeting on Thursday night and all day on Sunday — blessed periods of respite from daylong toil.

And Bradford and the Separatists were growing less clannish, less isolated. They grew more tolerant of others, so that by 1614, just a few years after they had moved to Leyden, Robinson suggested that it was legitimate to pray and read Scripture even with members of the Church of England; perhaps it was even permissible to join with them in the Lord's Supper. A few years earlier such a sentiment would have seemed unthinkable; it was still unthinkable for the bishops of the Church of England.

Yet it would be this very tolerance that would lead, among other things, to the Separatists' decision to leave Leyden, the "bewtifull citie" that had been so welcoming. As Robinson's congregation became more and more accepting of Dutch ways, so would it become less and less English. Every other Separatist congregation that came to the Netherlands was eventually absorbed by the Dutch and lost its identity; Bradford could see that this might happen to the congregation at Green Gate also. Already some of the Separatist children had entered the Dutch army or navy, and some — those who had no memories of England — saw the Netherlands as their native country. Within two or three generations, the English character of the group might well be completely gone. Despite their quarrel with the English church, the Separatists had no desire to deny their English heritage.

And there were other concerns. While the Separatists maintained their strict discipline on the Sabbath, listening to Pastor Robinson and Elder Brewster "ripping up the heart & conscience before God," their children looked around and saw the Dutch celebrating Sunday as a holiday. The Separatists watched their children, who had not been part of the fire of the earlier movement, being drawn "into extravagante & dangerous courses, getting the reins off their necks, & departing from their parents."

They were also concerned about their standard of living. By 1617, the Separatists had been in Leyden eight years, but even with constant, unwearying labor only a few had reached a comfortable living. Most remained poor, so poor that they were forced to send their children to work. This meant no education and a stunted childhood, and the Separatists grieved: "Though their minds were free and willing, yet their bodies bowed under the weight of the same and became decrepit in their early youth, the vigour of nature being consumed in the very bud." Friends back in England who might have moved to the freedom of Leyden were reluctant to come, recognizing that they might well live in poverty, with no support as they grew old or if their business failed or they fell sick. Even some of the congregation at Green Gate decided to return to England, since they "preferred & chose the prisons in England rather than this libertie in Holland, with these afflictions."

And there was yet another serious affliction for this people so frequently tried. In 1617, William Brewster decided the Separatist cause needed a printing press so that its ideas could be published and distributed; this would have been impossible in England, and even in Leyden it was dangerous. A decade later, Reverend Alexander Leighton, who had published pamphlets from abroad for this same cause, was captured in London and sentenced to a fine of ten thousand pounds — an amount he could not have paid in a lifetime. He was also whipped and pilloried, had one ear cut off and one nostril sliced, was branded on the cheek, and was finally sentenced to life imprisonment in London Fleet prison.

When, in 1619, Brewster anonymously published his *Perth Assembly,* which attacked King James for forcing Scottish Presbyterians to accept the rule of English bishops, James demanded that the author be arrested. He gave the job to the Dutch ambassador, who asked Dutch printers to identify the printer through examining the type. They correctly identified William Brewster, but when the Dutch agents employed by the ambassador raided Brewster's home, he had disappeared. He began hiding in one Separatist home after another, but as the manhunt continued month after month, Bradford and the others soon recognized that their elder would forever be a homeless fugitive as long as they remained in Leyden.

Perhaps the Separatists might have found ways to keep their vision alive, to avoid being absorbed into the Dutch culture. Perhaps they could have found a way to protect William Brewster. And perhaps, after a time, they might have begun to thrive in their trades. But the years were going by, and a ten-year truce the Dutch had drawn up with Spain was nearing its end. All the citizens of the Netherlands feared the revival of what had been a very bloody struggle, but none feared it more than the Separatists. If Spain should be the victor, it would mean that the Catholic Church would become the state church. The Inquisition would be established in the Netherlands, and would root out Separatists with intimidation and torture. The persecutions that Elizabeth and James had established in England would be fleabites in comparison.

The Separatists came to believe that their time in the Netherlands was nearing an end. If they wished to preserve their way of life — and perhaps their lives themselves — they would have to continue the pilgrimage they had begun so long ago. For Bradford, there were probably few regrets. After initial successes, he had suffered great financial loss, which he attributed to God for the good of his own soul.

But move on to where? There was Jamestown across the Atlantic, the colony that had been established in Virginia in 1607. But word had come back to England of the terrible hardships these colonists had endured, so terrible that it was becoming more and more difficult to persuade people to travel from England to join the colony. In 1616 King James was proposing that men condemned to death should be granted reprieves if only they would agree to journey to Virginia.

Others in Leyden thought of Guiana, situated on the northern coast of South America. The Separatists had read Sir Walter Raleigh's accounts of that land, what he called the "mighty rich and beautiful empire, and of that great and golden city, which the Spaniards call El Dorado." He spoke of the "assurance of riches and glory" as he described the lush forests and the hoards of gold. But in 1617, Raleigh had lost many of his men in the steamy jungle; if one group of Englishmen had succumbed to the climate, perhaps others would as well. This, together with Catholic Spain's ownership of Guiana, seems to have been enough to convince the Separatists to abandon this site.

Then there was New England. The Separatists had read of this land too, a land much like their homeland. Captain John Smith — the same man who had been rescued by Pocahontas down at Jamestown — had visited New England in 1614. Two years later he wrote of the "Fish and Furres," of the "goodnesse and greatness of those spacious Tracts of land," of the "excellent good Harbours," of land "overgrown with all sorts of excellent good woods for building houses . . . ; with an incredible abundance of most sorts of fish, much fowle, and sundry sorts of good fruites for mans use." "Who can but approve this a most excellent place," he concluded, "both for health and fertility?"

But the Separatist readers must have noticed the warning that John Smith included: "But it is not a worke for every one, to manage such an affaire as makes a discoverie, and plants a Colony. It requires all the best parts of Art, Judgement, Courage, Honesty, Constancy, Diligence, and Industrie, to do but near well."

In a sense, the Separatists had already proven themselves, and some, like Bradford, were confident. But others in Robinson's congregation disagreed. There were no funds for such a trip. The journey itself would be a hardship. The colony would have to fight off disease and starvation. And there were the Indians. The Separatists imagined them as "cruel, barbarous, & most trecherous," who did things that would make "the bowels of men to grate within them."

Bradford and others admitted the dangers; the difficulties were many, but not insurmountable. And this would not be a voyage in search of gold, or to claim a new territory, or merely to explore. "Their ends were good & honourable; their calling, lawful & urgent; and therefore they might expecte the blessing of God in their proceding. Yea, though they should lose their lives in this action, yet might they have comforte in the same. . . . All great & honourable actions are accompanied with great difficulties, and must be both enterprised and overcome with answerable courages."

The group decided to go.

They decided upon Virginia, but they would live apart from the Jamestown Colony, knowing that the Church of England was settled there as well. Now, in 1617, began three years of anxious and exhausting negotiations. If they would go, they needed the financial backing of a company like the London Company that had financed the Jamestown Colony. And they would need a patent from the king of England to settle his land. They hoped that if James had been willing to send convicts and the condemned to the New World, he would be willing to allow them to go as well.

To seek out the possibilities, the congregation sent John Carver, who would one day be the first governor of Plymouth Colony, and Robert Cushman, one of the deacons of the congregation, to England. Bradford was still too young in the leadership of the church to go, and Brewster's life would have been in danger. They crossed over from the Netherlands and approached the London Company, also known as the First Virginia Company, by seeking out Sir Edwin Sandys, an influential member of the Company who was friendly to the Separatist cause. The Company jumped at the chance. Here was a group of people actually willing to sail to Virginia; if they added to the health of a dying colony, it would mean profits both for the London Company and the king himself.

But there was a sticking point: the Separatists insisted upon a statement that would insure their religious freedom in the New World. Edwin Sandys assured Cushman and Carver that such a promise would not be difficult to obtain. The Company then promised the Separatists a tract of land in Virginia, with all the rights of local government. Sir Robert Naunton, the secretary of state, promised to obtain the patent from the king that would grant all the promises of the London Company and insure religious freedom. When the proposal was finally brought to the king, he seemed to agree enthusiastically. "What profits may arise in the parts to which they intend to go?" he asked, perhaps demonstrating why he was so enthusiastic. When he was told that they would be fishermen, the king declared, "So God have my soul, 'tis an honest trade. It was the Apostle's own calling."

But as so often happened with the Separatists, happy beginnings did not always lead to equally happy endings. The next day James suggested that the Separatists meet with the bishops from the Church of England to discuss their differences. The folk in Leyden, many of whom had visited British prisons, would have none of that. The result was that James would not issue the patent for reasons of state, though privately he promised that if the Separatists would go to Virginia even without the charter, he "would . . . not molest them, provided they carried themselves peaceably."

Cushman and Carver returned to Leyden with mixed news. With such wavering on the part of the king, the Leyden folk grew discouraged, or, as Bradford wrote, the wavering "made a dampe in the busines, and caused some distraction." With such a "sandy foundation," many argued, they could not proceed. But others like Bradford were not yet ready to yield, recognizing that it was God, and not the king, who would lead them in this new adventure. Besides, a charter with a "seale as broad as the house floor" was no guarantee; a king could revoke a charter at his whim. They must depend on God's providence, and not on the blessings of kings or bishops.

For two years, Cushman and Carver worked to obtain a patent to a tract of land to the north of the Virginia colony. In 1619 they returned to England and, hiding their identities, finally were able to take out a patent in the name of John Wincob, a preacher in the household of Dowager Duchess of London. He had said that he would accompany the Separatists in their venture, but when the time came, he never did. It mattered little, since the Separatists would never use the patent for which they had negotiated so long.

A view of the London Bridge, lined with the shops of merchants and craftsmen.
The Merchant Adventurers probably had businesses on this bridge.

Having secured the patent, however, the Separatists still had no financing for the voyage. The London Company was almost bankrupt, having had so many reverses at Jamestown. It could provide neither ships nor supplies. Then suddenly, in the beginning of 1620, a new offer came, this time from the New Netherlands Company. It promised free transportation, cattle for each of the families, and the same kind of religious freedom the Separatists had enjoyed in the Netherlands. In February, the officers of the Company asked the Prince of Orange to provide two warships that would protect the Separatists from the anger of the English king until the Separatists had settled. In return, all the New Netherlands Company asked was that the Separatists settle in the Dutch colony by the Hudson River, much farther north of Jamestown. Negotiations went well, and Brewster indicated to the Company that he had "the means of inducing over four hundred families to accompany him thither, both out of this country and England, provided they would be guarded and protected from all violence on the part of other potentates." Had a few more weeks passed, the history of New England would have been very different.

At the last moment, an ironmonger named Thomas Weston arrived at the Green Portal in Leyden. Learning of the Separatists' plans, he urged them not only to reject the offers of the London Company, but to reject as well the offers of the Dutch New Netherlands Company. He himself, together with a group of "Merchant Adventurers," would advance the money for the ship and the supplies the Separatists would need. Once they were established in the New World, the Separatists could then pay back the money they owed the Adventurers.

The negotiating for how this money was to be paid was long and hard. Weston proposed that the Separatists and the Merchant Adventurers each be given a certain number of "shares" in the colony. The colonists were to work entirely for the colony; this labor would provide them with all the provisions they needed. At the end of seven years, everything was to be divided among the Merchant Adventurers and the Separatists. The Separatists objected, offering to work only five days a week for the colony and claiming that their houses, "gardens, & home lots" should be exempt from the final division, otherwise they would be little more than servants. The discussions dragged on, the Separatists becoming angry with Weston, and Weston becoming angry with the Separatists.

The Separatists also had to decide who should go over first, since they at first believed that only eighty or ninety would go in an advance party. They judged that only the "youngest and the strongest part" should go, and only if they should volunteer. Since the majority of the Leyden congregation was to remain in the Netherlands, John Robinson would remain behind as pastor and William Brewster should go as ruling elder in the new colony; this arrangement also had the advantage of removing Brewster from King James's reach. If the colony succeeded, then those who remained, if "the Lord gave them life, & means, & opportunitie . . . would come to them as soone as they could." But if the colony should fail, those in Leyden would help the survivors return to their former home.

In the center of all of these decisions and negotiations was William Bradford. He and others were determined to make the voyage, and with Carver and Cushman still in London, and with William Brewster still hiding from King James, it is likely that Bradford was the one who made the careful preparations for the trip. The Separatists began to sell their properties in Leyden, Bradford selling the house for which he had waited so long to Jan des Obrys for 1,120 guilders. Farmers as they were, they knew they could not delay too long if they hoped to reach New England, build the houses, and plant the crops that they could harvest in the fall.

Still, it was June — already past planting time in New England — by the time the Merchant Adventurers chartered the 180-ton vessel that would take the Separatists to New England. At the same time, the Separatists, perhaps under Bradford's direction, used the money from the sale of their properties to purchase the *Speedwell,* a 60-ton vessel they felt would be useful at the colony in "fishing and shuch other affairs as might be for the good & benefite of the colonie." And such a ship could have been useful, not only in fishing, but also in exploring the coast and making trading runs.

However, farmers do not always make the best judgments about ships. Maybe the *Speedwell* needed a complete overhaul to make her seaworthy, or perhaps she was too overburdened by sails and so wrenched open while out at sea. But in either case the Sepa-

The Pilgrims setting out from Delftshaven, bound for Southampton

ratists could not have known that the choice of the *Speedwell* would prove disastrous.

June slipped into July, the month that crops should have been sprouting and growing; three weeks into that month John Robinson finally declared a "day of solemn humiliation," which was followed by a feast at his own house. This was the time of endings, for the next day some of the Separatists would set out and never again see those they had left behind. There was good eating, good drinking, and song, what Edward Winslow would remember later as "the sweetest melody that ever mine ears heard." Then came farewells, fitful sleep, final preparations, and, at dawn on July 21, 1620, the Separatists set out for Delftshaven, traveling by canal about twenty miles to the south. Some came from Leyden with them, and some

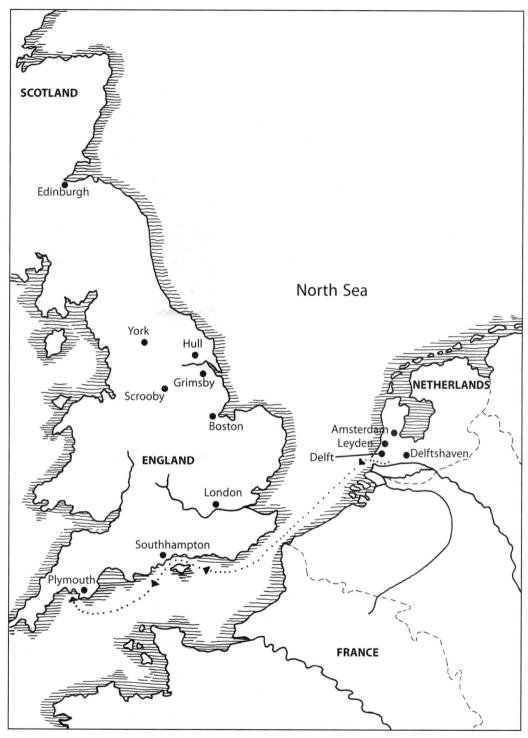

SCOTLAND

Edinburgh

North Sea

York

Hull

Grimsby

Scrooby

Boston

NETHERLANDS

Amsterdam

Leyden

Delft

Delftshaven

ENGLAND

London

Southhampton

Plymouth

FRANCE

The Pilgrims' journey from the Netherlands to England was dogged by troubles.

This drawing, similar to a seventeenth-century print of Southampton, shows the *Speedwell* and the *Mayflower* anchored in the harbor.

came all the way from Amsterdam, some fifty miles, to see them off. At Delftshaven there was another feast, more farewells, more prayer and song, and the next morning, the Separatists boarded the *Speedwell*. This is the group of Separatists who would later be known as the Pilgrims.

For William and Dorothy, it was a particularly wrenching time. Their son, John, was not to come. Perhaps they thought him delicate, as Bradford himself had been thought delicate at that age. Perhaps they thought the separation would not be long. Perhaps they left him in the care of the Robinsons, who expected to join this group shortly. But in the end, the parting was heartbreaking, much sharper than they could have imagined then.

50

John Robinson would never make it to the New World, but no one knew this on that July morning. He knelt on the pier and "with watery cheeks commended them with most fervente prayers to the Lord." Bradford remembered the scene with exquisite pain: "[T]ruly doleful was the sight of that sad and mournful parting, to see what sighs and sobs and prayers did sound amongst them, what tears did gush from every eye, & pithy speeches pierced each heart."

Finally it was time to go, and "with mutual embraces and many tears, they tooke their leaves one of another, which proved to be the last leave to many of them." And so they left the Netherlands, "but they knew they were pilgrimes, & looked not much on those things, but lifted up their eyes to the heavens, their dearest country, and quieted their spirits." It was this kind of sure vision, this kind of determination and confidence in God, that would stand Bradford in good stead in the task to come.

The journey to England was short, and the Pilgrims put in at Southampton, right beside the *Mayflower,* the ship that the Merchant Adventurers had hired. As Bradford peered from the *Speedwell*'s side, he was seeing his homeland for the first time in twelve years. He was eager to begin.

But nothing on this voyage happened quickly. The Pilgrims had to meet the fifty colonists in the group of "Strangers," people chosen by Thomas Weston for the skills they could bring a new colony: tanners, weavers, and shopkeepers. They had to negotiate a relationship with a soldier they had met and employed in the Netherlands: Miles Standish. And there were still negotiations to be conducted with Weston, who came down to Southampton to meet them and asked them to sign the agreement they had earlier rejected. The Pilgrims refused and asked for more funds. Weston, angry, left them, claiming that he would have no more to do with them (though he changed his mind later). Eventually the Pilgrims had to dip into their supplies, selling "some 3 or 4 score firkins of butter, which comoditie they might best spare" in order to clear their debts in the English port.

Finally, on August 5, when crops should have begun ripening in New England, the *Mayflower* and the *Speedwell* set out to sea. Bradford may have been on the *Speedwell* as one of the assistants to the ship's master; Robert Cushman, a Pilgrim, and Christopher Martin, a Stranger, were assistants on the *Mayflower*. It seemed that they were finally under way, but after only a few days, the *Speedwell* was "open and leakie as a sieve." At one place, Cushman complained, "the water came in as at a mole hole." The ships turned and put in at Dartmouth, and just in time, according to Cushman, for if she had "stayed at sea but 3 or 4 hours more, she would have sunke right downe."

Bradford must have worried again about the loss of time and the resolve of the Pilgrims. And clearly many of the passengers had lost faith in the journey, so that Martin ordered that everyone aboard the *Mayflower* should be kept on board and would not "suffer them to goe ashore lest they should run away." Cushman was disgusted, but noted that "God can do much, & his will be done." Repairs took two more weeks. Already some crops — corn, especially — could have been harvested in New England.

They set out again, but three hundred miles beyond Land's End, three hundred miles out into the Atlantic, there was another problem. The *Speedwell*, even after repairs, was "so leakie as he must bear up or sinke at sea," complained the captain, "for they could scarce free her with much pumping." They turned back east yet again, sailing into Plymouth to have the *Speedwell* repaired. After being searched from stem to stern, no specific fault was found in the

Sailing to the New World aboard the *Mayflower*

ship, and Bradford attributed the leaks to "generall weaknes." They decided to leave it behind — where in later years it would be refitted in London and sail on many a voyage.

But now came another crisis: if the *Speedwell* was to be left behind, then all of the passengers would need to go on the *Mayflower;* it could not hope to hold as many. Twenty people had to abandon the journey — some gratefully, such as Robert Cushman, who in addition to worrying about leaks, had been terribly seasick. Others left out of fear for the well-being of their children, and others still left "out of some discontente or feare they conceived of the ill success of the voyage, seeing so many crosses befall & the year time so far spent." Some of these must have recognized as well that leaving behind the *Speedwell* meant that the fishing the Pilgrims had planned to undertake, the fishing that would be the backbone of their provisions and the way in which they would earn the money to pay the Merchant Adventurers, was now going to be impossible. In the end, only three members of the original Scrooby congregation left on the *Mayflower:* William and Mary Brewster, and William Bradford.

More time lost. More supplies used up even before arrival in the New World. It was not until September 6 that Bradford could look back to the east and see England fading over the horizon, or look to the west and see the expanse of ocean that lay between him and the New World. As the ship sped along under a "fine small gale," he must have been pleased that he was finally under way.

In New England, most of the crops that could have been planted would have now been harvested.

FOUR

"After Longe Beating at Sea"

Afine east-northeast wind took the *Mayflower* quickly out of view of land, and the captain must have wished the wind would continue so; he knew they were close to the equinox and its storms. If Bradford was praying for the wind to continue, his prayers were answered, as they blew the boat out to the middle of the Atlantic. But these same winds also chopped up the seas, so that soon the passengers were terribly seasick.

But there was little room to be privately miserable. The *Mayflower* had two decks. The main deck held a poop house and forecastle, which housed the crew of thirty. The passengers lived on the lower deck, and below them were holds for cargo, water casks, sail lockers, and all the supplies. The *Mayflower* had in the past hauled fish, timber, and tar from Norway, and then, most recently, casks of wine from Bordeaux and Gascony. But carrying wine and timber is one thing; carrying passengers another. In the area between decks, 102 souls tried to be comfortable. It was not easy. In fact, there was

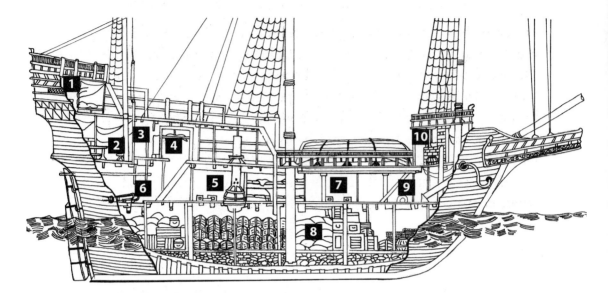

A cross-section of the *Mayflower II*, a modern recreation of the original ship

1. **The Round House** is the chartroom where the ship's progress is planned and plotted.

2. **The Great Cabin** houses the commander of the ship.

3. **The Whipstaff** is a long lever used to move the tiller below, which moves the rudder to steer the ship.

4. **The Steerage** is the cabin for the ship's officers.

5. **The Capstan** is a type of winch or pulley used to hoist cargo.

6. **The Gun Room** held two guns called minions, kept ready to defend against attack.

7. **The 'tween decks** houses the passengers.

8. **The Hold** is the main cargo space.

9. **The Windlass** is used for raising anchors.

10. **The Forecastle** houses the common seamen and the cook. Meals for the crew were prepared here.

not enough room for all the passengers to lie down together; some may have slept in the shallop, the small boat aboard the *Mayflower*. The space allowed for no beds, so the passengers must have slept on hammocks or on the deck itself, perhaps on pallets they had brought along. There were a few "cabbins," and probably these private places went to the married couples, including Bradford and Dorothy.

The cook's galley was all the way forward — this so that the wind, coming from behind, would blow the galley's smoke away from the ship — and it was only adequate for the crew's meals. This meant that passenger meals were mostly cold, probably biscuit, salt beef that had been soaked in fresh water to remove some of the salt, cheese, and beer. Occasionally there would have been fish, which would have been cooked over an open charcoal fire carefully set in a pit of sand; with so much tar around the wooden ship, there was always the danger of fire.

Soon after this voyage, all of the Pilgrims would look to Bradford as someone they could trust, someone who could govern and make just and prudent decisions. This reputation may have begun on board the *Mayflower*, perhaps when Bradford negotiated the relationships between the various groups of passengers. So many people in such a small space often breeds ill feelings, and this happened aboard the *Mayflower*. The Leyden Pilgrims felt they were in charge of the voyage; to this, the Strangers objected. Part of this came about as both sides felt a growing sense that they were all equal in this venture — a democratic spirit that would be important in Plymouth.

Somehow Bradford was also able to earn the respect of the Strangers, a respect which would never diminish during his life. Though Bradford must have spent a great deal of time with his old friend Brewster, who had been in hiding for over a year, and with others from the Leyden congregation — John Carver, who would

Miles Standish, who
became one of
Bradford's close friends

become Plymouth's first governor, the deacon Samuel Fuller, and
Edward Winslow — he also grew to know some of the leading
Strangers. He met men like John Alden, who would later marry
Priscilla Mullins. He was, as Bradford remembered him, a "hopeful
younge man." Alden was ten years younger than Bradford, and on
board was employing his trade as a cooper, responsible for checking
their barrels of beer, fresh water, and "strong water" to be sure that
they remained airtight. Bradford also met Strangers like Richard
Warren, whom he dubbed "a usefull instrumente," and Stephen
Hopkins, the only man among all the passengers who had been to
the New World before.

Bradford would also deepen his friendship with Miles Standish, a professional soldier four or five years older than he was. He was short, and his red hair and red complexion suggested his fiery temper. He had been to the Netherlands with the troops that England had sent to fight against the Spanish, and sometime during his tour of duty, or perhaps soon after, he had met John Robinson. However, he remained apart from the Separatist cause and never became a part of the church at Plymouth Colony.

To Bradford fell the task of negotiating relationships between passengers and the ship's crew. The crew of the *Mayflower* seemed to have little respect for the passengers, and set about "cursing them dayly with grievous execrations." One "lustie sea-man" particularly enjoyed tormenting the sickened Pilgrims, telling them that he would bury half of them at sea and then "make merry with what they had." When the Pilgrims rebuked him, "he would curse & swear most bitterly." But the Pilgrims would later use him as a sign. One morning he was sick himself, and by the end of the afternoon his body had been cast over the side. Bradford noted, with some satisfaction, that the other sailors took note of this death, for they saw — undoubtedly, the Pilgrims pointed this out as well — that his terrible death was "the just hand of God upon him."

The *Mayflower* was not a fast ship, averaging about two miles an hour on her long journey to the west. The captain — and Bradford — must have yearned for a quicker passage, but it was not to be. Halfway across the Atlantic, the storms of the equinox, which they might have avoided had they left England on schedule, caught up to them. The captain confined the Pilgrims below the decks, as the sailors left the masts bare — the wind would have ripped the sails to shreds in seconds — and tried to keep the ship heading into the waves so that she would not be broached, with the waves knocking her over on her side, or pooped, with the waves catching up to her from behind and swamping her stern.

The ship, Bradford wrote, was "shrewdly shaken," and the seams of the decks opened. Frigid water cascaded down upon the Pilgrims, already badly frightened by a storm the likes of which they had never seen on land. For days on end they shivered in the cold and wet, breathing bad air, confined with no chance of exercise, eating unhealthy food; many grew ill.

One young man, John Howland, ventured up onto the deck; perhaps he simply could not remain below any longer. Immediately the ship pitched and threw him overboard, "but it pleased God that he caught hold of the top-saile halliards, which hung over board, and ran out at length; yet he held his hold (though he was sundrie fathoms under water) till he was hauled up by the same rope to the brim of the water, and then with a boat hooke and other means got into the shipe againe, and his life spared." Bradford was always aware that God's hand was upon them, whether in the death of the "lustie sea-man" or the saving of Howland, another "lustie younge man."

The storms stretched one into another, and it seemed that the ship would indeed be lost: with the strain of the waves, the main beam in the middle of the ship first bowed, then cracked. It was a desperate time. The sailors themselves were not sure how to proceed; some argued that they were halfway across and should go on, while others "were loath to hazard their lives too desperately." The Pilgrims must have wondered if they would return yet again to England.

But Bradford, confident in God's providence, must not have been surprised when one of the Leyden folk proposed placing an immense iron screw under the cracked beam and forcing it back

The *Mayflower II* under sail — in considerably better condition than the
original *Mayflower* when it neared the New World

into its correct position. The ship's carpenter agreed: they could screw the beam back, set a post under it with firm footings on the lower deck, and it would be "sufficiente." As this repair was under way, the sailors began to caulk the seams again, and "though with the workeing of the ship they would not longe keepe stanch, yet ther would otherwise be no great danger, if they did not overpress her with sails" — something they must have learned from the loss of the *Speedwell.*

If the ship was "sufficiente," it was just barely so. The storms were continuing, and the post provided a makeshift repair only. The waves continued to open up the seams, and the passengers had no relief. Still, "they committed them selves to the will of God, and re-solved to proseede." There was their answerable courage.

Though this rough handling likely caused many a death in the first year of Plymouth Colony, only one passenger died during the voyage: William Button, the servant of Samuel Fuller, twenty-two years old. He died within sight of his hope as "they drew near the coast." But the number of passengers would remain the same, for Stephen and Elizabeth Hopkins gave birth to a son. They named him after his homeplace: Oceanus.

Sixty-six days and sixty-six nights they sailed, wondering if they would ever see the coast of the New World. Finally, on November 10, 1620, a Friday, "after long beating at sea they fell with that land which is called Cape Cod." Once the captain confirmed the location from his charts, "they were not a little joyfull."

When Bradford looked out across to the shore, he was looking at the very wrist of Cape Cod, at what is now called Truro. A long expanse of sandy shoreline stretched down to the south; heading inland the land rose to some low bluffs, the dunes held in place by the scrub pines that are still to be found there. Had the Pilgrims landed and climbed the bluffs, they could have seen what is now known as Cape Cod Bay to the west, and beyond that another shoreline — if the day was very clear — that would become most familiar to them.

It was land. It was not the land for which they had a patent to settle, but it was land. Every eye on the ship must have feasted on it, thanking God for their safe arrival.

But after conferring, they agreed with Captain Jones that the *Mayflower* should turn south so that they might settle somewhere past the mouth of the Hudson River, a site that would be part of the English patent and therefore legal; the Hudson would also give them ready access to the country's interior. And so, after nine and a half weeks at sea, the Pilgrims turned away from their landfall to search for a better place. But all the while, the land remained visible off to starboard.

After sailing half a day, they arrived at the elbow of Cape Cod and what was then known as Tucker's Terror, today Pollack's Rip. Either name suggests the possibilities. "They fell amongst dangerous shoulds and roaring breakers, and they were so far entangled ther with as they conceived them selves in great danger." With the wind starting to die away, the ship, instead of putting out to sea and losing sight of land again to go around the breakers, turned north, went back past Truro, and above the fist of Cape Cod. After standing off and on all night, they put into the shelter of what would later be called Provincetown harbor around mid-morning. There was no more exploring southward.

The Pilgrims' first response to this landfall was one of thanksgiving. "Being thus arived in a good harbor and brought safe to land, they fell upon their knees and blessed the God of heaven, who had brought them over the vast and furious ocean, and delivered them from all the periles and miseries therof, againe to set their feete on the firme and stable earth, their proper elemente."

But this joy was mixed with real terror. Behind them lay a vast expanse of ocean which separated them from any supplies. They could expect little help from the *Mayflower* itself. Already the supplies were running low and the sailors were insisting that the Pilgrims land so that they could turn back and reach England before they had consumed all their food; in fact, some of the sailors were muttering that the Pilgrims should simply be turned off the ship.

Nor did the sandy shore hold much hope out to these farmers and tradesmen. "[T]hey had no friends to wellcome them, nor inns to entertaine or refresh their weatherbeaten bodys, no houses or much less townes to repaire too, to seeke for succoure." In short, this was quite different from their arrival in Amsterdam so long ago.

But it was worse than this: not only was there nothing to welcome them, but the land itself seemed hostile. "For summer being done, all things stand upon them with a wetherbeaten face; and the whole countrie, full of woods and thickets, represented a wild and savage hue." In fact, with winter coming on it would be difficult to explore to find a suitable place to settle, for the winters were "sharp and violent, and subjecte to cruell and fierce stormes, dangerous to travel to known places, much more to search an unknown coast."

And there was always the fear, perhaps rarely mentioned aloud, of the Indians. Even if they could explore in the winter, Bradford wrote, "what could they see but a hideous and desolate wildernes, full of wild beast and wild men? And what multituds ther might be of them they knew not." These were certainly fears that the Pilgrims must have had even before leaving Leyden. But now, having arrived at the coast, those fears were suddenly very real and very close. Their response to this fear was the same as their response to all the fears that had troubled them for so long: Seeing that they could find no solace in the things around them, they cast their eyes "upward to the heavens," for "what could now sustaine them but the spirite of God and his grace?"

If the fears overwhelmed some, they did not overwhelm Bradford. He hoped that his children — and the children of all the fathers on that voyage — could say,

> Yea, let them which have been redeemed of the Lord, shew how he hath delivered them from the hand of the oppressour. When they wandered in the deserte willdernes out of the way, and found no citie to dwell in, both hungrie, and thirstie, their sowle was overwhelmed in them. Let them confess before the Lord his loving kindness, and his wonderfull works before the sons of men.

Like the Hebrew children who had wandered so long in the desert wilderness, the Pilgrims were coming to set up a new country, a new way of living. And they trusted in God to see it established.

And like the Hebrews, this was not a united group; the "Saints" — Pilgrims from the Leyden congregation — and the Strangers were still not one people, facing together the challenge of establishing a successful colony. There were "discontents & murmurings amongst some, and mutinous speeches & carriages in others." Since they had put down at Cape Cod, and not in Virginia, some of the Strangers claimed the patent was no longer valid, and that neither the Leyden group, nor any other, had the right to govern the colony. Some of the Strangers had bragged that they would "use their own libertie" once they reached land, and certainly some, especially the poorer among them and the servants, might have felt that here in New England "none had power to command them" and they need not slave for the Merchant Adventurers.

At this point, Bradford must have remembered the advice of Pastor Robinson, that gentle man whose presence would so often be

The signing of the Mayflower Compact

missed in the coming months. In a farewell letter, he had told the Leyden folk that, together with the Strangers, they should form a "body politik," which meant a single unity that could stand together against the dangers that the sandy shore presented. It was a new idea to Bradford, that a group of people could form their own government and choose how they would appoint their own leaders. It meant that the people would govern themselves, that their leaders would be accountable to the people that chose them, that the people would voluntarily agree to be governed. No one aboard the *Mayflower* had ever lived under such a system before.

And so the document now known as the Mayflower Compact was drawn up, probably by William Brewster. Bradford called it "a combination," and perhaps that word is more precise, since it led to a combination of settlers; no one was higher than another, no one was seen as more important, and all were equally responsible in the colony. When it was completed, all the men were called into the

Signatures of the *Mayflower* Pilgrims

cabin of John Carver and the document was read aloud. What they heard was the voice of democracy.

> In the name of God, Amen. We whose names are underwritten, the loyall subjects of our dread soveraigne Lord, King James . . . do by these presents solemnly & mutually in the presence of God, and one of another, covenant & combine ourselves togeather into

a civill body politick . . . and by vertue hearof to enacte, consti-
tute, and frame such just & equall lawes, ordinances, acts, consti-
tutions, & offices, from time to time, as shall be thought most
meete & convenient for the generall good of the Colonie, unto
which we promise all due submission and obedience.

After the reading, the Saints and Strangers chose John Carver as the
first governor of the colony — the first time in the New World that
any colonists had chosen their own governor. And with that, all the
murmurings and discontent, Bradford writes, "were soone quelled
and overcome by the wisdome, patience, and just and equall
carrage" of the governor.

Bradford, astute as he was, would have recognized that three
very important things had just happened. First, the Saints and
Strangers were now one body. Second, the Leyden group had in-
sured that its vision of the colony would not be diffused by the
Strangers, even though there were more Strangers than Saints. And
finally, there would be no more talk of moving elsewhere, of heading south to the Hudson River.

Now the colonists would need to find a place to settle. But it was
now noon on November 11, a Saturday — not the time to begin explorations with the Sabbath so close at hand. A small party of sixteen men went ashore, but just long enough to gather firewood.
They returned with hopeful reports. Sunday was set aside as a day of
rest and worship; the Leyden folk made no exception to this un-
breakable law, and after the Mayflower Compact, none of the
Strangers murmured against it. Finally, on Monday, November 13,
the Pilgrims landed on Cape Cod, having been eager "againe to set
their feete on the firme and stable earth, their proper elemente."

The women set to washing and airing their clothes, something they had not been able to do for the whole of the voyage. The children ran up and down the beach. Some of the men stood guard, while others brought ashore the ship's shallop — a small boat that could be either rowed or rigged with a mast — to repair the damage done by the mid-Atlantic storms. On the beach they found shellfish, clams, and mussels, which must have tasted extraordinary after nine weeks of salt beef and biscuit. Unfortunately, the feast was too rich for most, and the shellfish took their toll and made them "to cast and scour."

After two days, it was clear that the shallop would need many repairs. The Pilgrims felt it too dangerous to explore, but some in the party were so eager that they were finally "permitted" to do so. All were volunteers. On Wednesday, November 15, sixteen men set out. Miles Standish was in command, though he had an advisory group. One of these was William Bradford — the first of the Scrooby congregation to explore the interior. He was already showing the kind of leadership that would be so necessary to the colony.

About a mile down the beach, the Pilgrims came upon what they had feared so dreadfully: they saw five or six "salvages" with their dog. The Indians immediately fled into the woods. The Pilgrims rushed forward to try to speak with them; had they been able to, the next few weeks might have been easier for them.

Suspicious of the Indians and wanting to see "if there might not be more of them lying in ambush," the Pilgrims did the most foolish thing they could have done: though none of them had ever been in a wilderness like this, they rushed into the woods. The Indians, after some time, came back out onto the beach and rushed away, easily outdistancing the Pilgrims, who had had so little exercise for such a long time. However, they did leave a clear trail, and this Bradford and the others followed until nightfall, when they set up camp and posted their sentinels. It was probably an uneasy sleep.

Bradford was to become a most extraordinary governor, but there is no indication that he was a notable woodsman. When morning came, they wandered after the trail on the beach, but once the trail turned inland, they lost both it and themselves, "falling into such thickets as were ready to tear their cloaths & armore to pieces." But the thickets were not the only thing to plague Bradford. They came upon a tree "where a young Spritt was bowed downe over a bow, and some Acornes strewed under-neath"; it was a trap, obviously set there to catch a deer. As they passed, each of the men looked at it, until "William Bradford being in the Reare, when he came looked also upon it, and as he went about, it gave a sudden jerk up, and he was immediately caught by the leg: It was a very pretty device, made with a Rope of their owne making, and having a noose as artificially made, as any Roper in England can make." It was a tale that Bradford probably heard told more often than he wished.

They had been all morning without anything to drink. Finally, they came upon a spring, "being the first New-England water they drunke of, and was now in thir great thirste as pleasante unto them as wine or bear had been in for-times." It was also the first fresh water they had had for ten weeks. They drank, and continued their wanderings. They passed from the bay side of Cape Cod all the way over to the ocean side, and then meandered back again, passing a pond of clear water, one of the glacial ponds still to be seen on Cape Cod.

They began to pass signs of the Indians who lived here. They came upon cleared cornfields, then the remains of a house with a kettle. By one of the clearings they found heaps of sand raised up, and since they were out to explore, they dug into the heaps. Finding rotted arrows and an old bow, they concluded — correctly, as it turned out — that this was a burial site, and quickly they covered it back up. "[I]t would be odious unto them," Bradford said, "to ran-

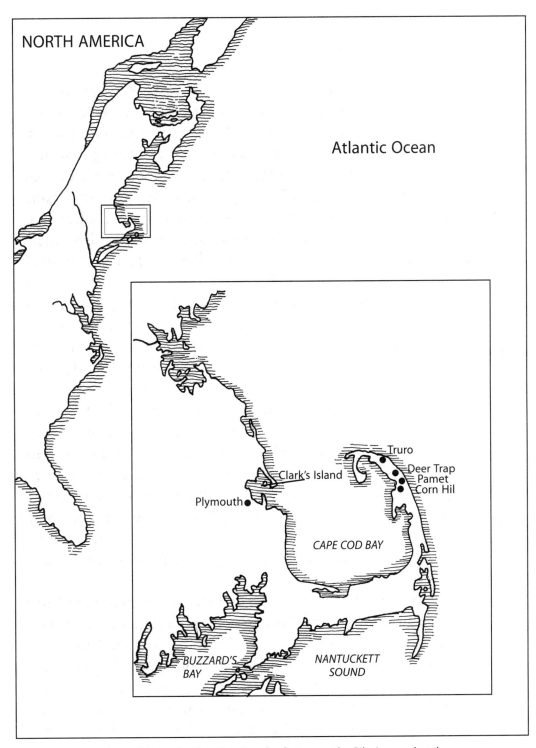

NORTH AMERICA

Atlantic Ocean

Truro
Deer Trap
Pamet
Corn Hil
Clark's Island
Plymouth

CAPE COD BAY

BUZZARD'S
BAY

NANTUCKETT
SOUND

Map of Cape Cod Bay showing the first areas the Pilgrims explored

sack their sepulchres." From there they searched for a river whose mouth they had seen from their ship; it might provide a harbor, as well as a way to the interior. In short, it might be a place where they could settle.

To find the river, they returned to the beach and began walking back toward their original landing site. On the way, they came upon a meadow at the base of a tall sandy hill, and again heaps of sand were mounded about, one clearly recent. Despite the possibility that these might be more graves, the Pilgrims began to excavate and found something startling: corn. The kernels were huge, much larger than any they had seen in England, even in the best growing years. And there were so many exotic colors, "which seemed to them a very goodly sight, (haveing never seen any shuch before)."

They named the spot Corn Hill, and, having posted guards to be sure that the Indians would not attack, they dug up the seed corn that had been so carefully stored there for the next season. If they had any qualms about this, they said to themselves that here was the providence of God, providing a crop for the needs of the colonists. "But the Lord," Bradford wrote, "is never wanting unto his in their greatest needs; let his holy name be praised."

When they found the river for which they had been searching — today it is named the Pamet — they discovered it to be a tidal river in which the shallop could indeed be harbored. They returned, undoubtedly to a boatload of people who were anxiously awaiting them, none more anxious, perhaps, than Dorothy.

Their news was exhilarating, but they returned to more murmurings and discontent. The *Mayflower* crew was grumbling about the delay, fearing now not only short supplies, but winter storms. The passengers, confined in the *Mayflower* with land just in sight, were eager and ready to begin; with winter coming on, they knew that a site had to be chosen and shelters built quickly. This would be made all the more difficult as the shallop still was not repaired, and thus not useful yet for explorations. In the next day or so it began to snow and the ground was quickly covered and frozen, so much so that had they not gone on their first trip of exploration, they would never have found the corn.

That seed corn represented a huge temptation for the Pilgrims. They had brought barley and peas, but no seed corn of their own, thinking their economy would be based principally on fishing and trade. But now, within reach lay an entire crop — something that might prove essential to the success of the colony.

They waited for a week as the shallop was repaired and as the snow continued to fall, and then Bradford set out with thirty-two other men, nine of whom were from the *Mayflower's* crew, presumably along to manage the shallop. Once again they found corn and, this time, beans of many colors, and once again they took them, but they resolved that they would pay for these — as they did, six months later when they had made contact with the Indians. "And here is to be noted a special providence of God, and a great mercie to this poore people," wrote Bradford, "that here they got seed to plant them corne the next year, or else they might have starved, for they had none, nor any liklyhood to get any till the season had been past."

Despite their good intentions about the corn, they seemed to have lost their scruples about the gravesites. They opened several, finding in one the skeletons of a child and of a man, the skull with "fine yellow hair still on it" — perhaps the body of a European sailor whom the Indians had tenderly buried. They found bowls, trinkets, a knife, beads, and some iron in the graves, and they removed "sundrie of the prettiest things." They also came upon Indian houses, from which the owners had apparently just fled. They found in them some food — herring and venison — as well as beautifully made baskets made of both fiber and crab shells. Here again, they took "some of the best things" away with them.

It seemed that Corn Hill might be the best spot to establish the colony. They could build the town on the hill, thus giving themselves a good defensive position. The Pamet would be close by, a good place to anchor the shallop. The ground was obviously fertile, and the bay would likely provide good fishing. Captain Jones assured them that with the proper gear, the bay alone would provide enough fish to pay off the Pilgrims' debt to the Merchant Adventurers in just two years instead of seven.

But others pointed out a fatal problem: there was no fresh water nearby. The clear ponds they had seen might dry up in the summer, and, in any case, if they built the town on the hill all the supplies, as well as the water, would have to be lugged up a steep path. Some suggested sailing north to Cape Ann to see if a likely spot might be found. But Robert Coppin, one of the sailors who had been in the bay before, spoke of a site directly across the bay — "Thievish Harbor," as it was called. Discussion dragged on, and days went by, and snow and cold continued.

It was now mid-December, and the decision was made to explore Coppin's site. Eighteen men gathered in the shallop, including Bradford, and set off on a typical New England winter day: "The weather was very could and it frose so hard as the sprea of the sea lighting on their coats, they were as if they had been glased." Turning the elbow of the Cape late in the day, they came upon a group of ten or twelve Indians working on something large and black on the beach. The Indians ran away, and as it was too late to explore, the Pilgrims landed and set up a barricade of logs and pine boughs.

In the morning, they found what the Indians had been working on: a grampus, a fish fifteen feet long covered with "some 2 inches thike of fat, like a hogg, . . . and fleshed like a swine." They explored into the woods and came upon another burial ground "like a churchyard, with young spires four or five yards long, set as close one by another as they could." Perhaps it reminded them of their own churchyards at home, for they "digged none of them up." This exploration took much of the day, so they moved the shallop just a few miles down to a small stream and again set up a barricade.

That night, the Pilgrims fired their first shots in the New World. Hearing a howling in the woods, they shot off two muskets until one of the sailors assured them that it was only the howling of wolves. In any case, the gunshots made the howling cease.

In the morning, however, the sailor was proved wrong. "All on the sudain, they heard a great & strange crie, which they knew to be the same voyces they had heard in the night, though they varied their notes." One of the sentries dashed in over the barricade, followed by arrows. Standish and one other man fired their flintlocks, while the others dashed across to the shallop to recover the guns they had recklessly left there.

When the Indians burst from the woods to cut these men off, Standish and others ran out, armed only with their cutlasses. Soon the men had reached the boat and "let flye amongst them, and quickly stopped their violence." One Indian, bolder than all the others, stayed close and shot arrow after arrow into the barricade, until Standish put a shot just by him; turning, he "gave an extraordinary shriek, and away they went all of them."

God had delivered them, Bradford wrote, and by his providence "not any one of them were either hurte, or hitt, though their arrows came close by them, and on every side them, and sundry of their coatse, which hunge up in the barricado, were shot throw and

Observing the Sabbath on Clark's Island

throw." None of the Indians were hurt either, something Bradford would be equally thankful for several months later.

But their dangers were not over. They set off again, and though the morning was a fair one, by mid-afternoon a gale blew so strong that it broke the rudder of the shallop, "& it was as much as 2 men could doe to steere her with a couple of oares." The sea grew and grew, so that finally the mast snapped in three places and the sailors had to cut it down and throw it overboard. But Coppin was confident: "Be of good cheer," he called, as in the growing darkness he recognized the landmarks that he expected would take them into the harbor. But suddenly the shoreline — and the white breakers that marked it — was all unfamiliar to him. "Lord, be merciful unto us, for mine eyes have never seen this place before."

"If you are men, about with her, or else we are all cast away," shouted one of the sailors, and so they worked the boat out to safety,

that marked it — was all unfamiliar to him. "Lord, be merciful unto us, for mine eyes have never seen this place before."

"If you are men, about with her, or else we are all cast away," shouted one of the sailors, and so they worked the boat out to safety, finally coming to place where a forested spit of land sheltered them from the wind. They decided to stay in the boat that night, since it was now dark and they could not be sure of safety. But it became so cold so quickly that some waded through the icy sea and lit a fire, so that "the rest were glad to come to them."

In the morning, they found they were on an island, Clark's Island as they named it, after the man who had first gone ashore. They were too tired to explore, so they dried their supplies and cleaned their muskets, and gave "God thanks for his mercies, in their manifould deliverances." Then they prepared for the Sabbath.

Finally, on Monday, December 11, a month after they had arrived in the New World, Bradford and the others went ashore to the mainland, sounding the harbor that lay between it and Clark's Island and discovering that it would accommodate ships. Bradford's last sight of England had been the town of Plymouth; he perhaps did not know, as he stepped ashore, that this very site had been described in 1614 by John Smith in his *Description of New England.* Six years earlier, he had named the place Plymouth. Bradford would have seen God's hand in this as well.

FIVE

Plymouth

If there was little to remind them of their homes in England — and even less to remind them of their homes in the Netherlands — still, Plymouth was the first spot they had seen that would suit for a colony. Bradford must have been eager by this time to have his own house again and to establish the home he and Dorothy had once had. On crossing the shore, the explorers marched up into the wooded high ground, and it seemed right away that the site was at least satisfactory. They found "diverse cornfields, and litle running brooks, a place (as they supposed) fitt for situation; at least it was the best they could find, and the season, and their presente necessitie, made them glad to accepte of it." Ready water, cleared fields, a good harbor — all seemed well.

The group hurried back across the bay, eager to tell of their find. Bradford, who had been a part of all three exploring parties, must have been particularly satisfied. After six weeks of beating about Cape Cod Bay, they were finally going to settle, and the adventure would truly begin.

But for Dorothy, Bradford's young wife, the adventure was over. When Bradford climbed aboard, he was told — perhaps by Brewster — that Dorothy had drowned. Had she fallen over the side, perhaps striking her head? Had she despaired at the bleak landscape she now watched from the *Mayflower?* Had she been terribly lonely, missing her son who was now an ocean away, and cut off from her husband who was so busy with the affairs of the colonists? Had she taken her own life?

To this day, no one knows. But Bradford could not — or would not — mourn. He seems to have felt that she had somehow failed him. Or perhaps he did not allow himself the chance to mourn, since there was so much to do in the colony. Or perhaps he kept himself busy so that he would not despair over her death. The only thing he did to mark her death was to note, under the column marked "Deaths" in his pocket notebook, the passing of "Dorothy, Wife to Mr. William Bradford." There is no record of him ever speaking her name again, not even to her son, who would eventually join him in Plymouth.

Three days passed as the Pilgrims, perhaps chastened by Dorothy's death, tried to decide what to do about settling. Finally, with the breeze blowing stiffly from the northwest, Captain Jones headed the *Mayflower* for Plymouth. But with the wind in that quarter, he could not work into the harbor; he had to wait until the next day to try again, vexed, along with his sailors, at the many delays on this journey. Finally the wind shifted and he sailed in, but as it was Saturday, the Pilgrims prepared for the next day's Sabbath services instead of going ashore. Captain Jones must have been chagrined.

The Pilgrims had indeed chosen an almost perfect site, though they had come at a time of year which could hardly have been worse.

It was an enclosed harbor, two spits of wooded and duned land jutting out from the mainland to batter down the waves. Though a ship could not enter with a northwest wind, it still had Cape Cod Bay to protect it while it waited for a shift. A fine, sandy beach led up to higher, dry ground, watered with streams and divided by the Town Brook that ran well inland. The ground was well suited to crops; a number of cleared fields would be good places to begin farms. At the same time, the wood was plentiful.

On Monday, a party landed in the shallop and marched seven or eight miles inland along the channels. They knew good farmland when they saw it, even if it was covered with new snow. The soil was "fat in some places," and the woods were full of pine and walnut for houses and furniture, and birch and hazel and sassafras for medicines. There were all sorts of berries, evidence of herbs, and a "great store of leeks and onions." And to build, they found sand, gravel, and clay, "no better in the world, excellente for pots, and will wash like soap; and great store of stone, though somewhat soft."

The next day, still not sure of their site, they sailed the shallop up the channel, a "very pleasant river," and found yet another site. But Bradford was practical-minded. He saw that the woods were thicker there, that there would be no cleared fields and no protection from the kind of Indian attacks that he had so recently seen. He argued, with others, for Clark's Island, the site which would provide the most protection for the Pilgrims. They returned down the river and explored the island once more, but found it unlikely to support the colony.

It was now Wednesday, December 20, and the Pilgrims decided to do what they usually did when faced with difficulties: they "called on God for direction." And with those prayers, and with the recognition that supplies were running low — "especially our Beere" — and with winter coming on, and with an impatient captain and crew, the Pilgrims decided to settle at what would become Plymouth, on the coast. Their reasons were a combination of practical considerations:

> [T]here is a great deale of Land cleared, and hath been planted with Corne three or four years agoe; and there is a very sweet brooke runnes under a hill side . . . where we may habour our boats and shallops exceeding well, and in this brooke much good fishe in their seasons; on the further side of the river also, much Corne ground cleared. In one field is a great hill on which we poynt to make a platforme & plant our Ordinance, which will command all round about.

Most of these reasons dealt with food. But the "Ordinance," or cannon, dealt with something very different: defense.

There was yet another advantage to this spot that the Pilgrims were unaware of. The Pawtuxet Indians who had once lived here had been wiped out by smallpox, and now no other tribe was eager to move into this area, fearing the disease. Had the Pilgrims landed anywhere else up or down the coast, the native tribes may have been much less willing to allow the colony to be established, and may easily have destroyed them, especially in their first year.

But even after they decided where to land, there were still more delays. Bradford, eager for work and dreading idle hours, must have been especially eager to begin. On that Wednesday when the decision was made, twenty men stayed ashore to begin building houses. Almost immediately a storm came upon them, even before the shallop could bring them food. A cold rain drenched them, and when the shallop came the next day, the storm was so bad that the boat had to be beached for two days.

Out in Cape Cod Bay, the *Mayflower* was tossed like a cork, so that when Mary Allerton gave birth to the journey's second child, it

The Pilgrims begin coming ashore by shallop.
This woodcut records the landing of John Alden and Mary Chilton.

was "dead borne." (She would follow her child in death about two months later.) Then it was Saturday and time to begin Sabbath preparations, these broken only by "the crie of some salvages, as they thought." And then it was Christmas Day — not a holiday the Leyden folk celebrated, and it seems that they squelched any celebration on the part of the Strangers.

But it was on this Christmas Day, 1620, that the colony of Plymouth (originally called "New Plimoth") truly began. Despite a "sore storm of wind & raine," all the men went ashore, "some to fell timber, some to saw, some to rive, and some to carry, so no man rested all that day." Perhaps they were simply eager to be out of the ship.

Raising the frame on a
post-and-beam house
(reenactment photo)

Slowly, slowly, Plymouth began to take shape, hampered by the cold, the weather, the mile and a half ride by boat back and forth to the *Mayflower,* and sickness. A road was laid out from the shore directly up a hill, then called The Mount, today called Burial Hill and still a steep climb. The men laid out nineteen narrow lots along this street and then began to build the nineteen small cottages that were to hold one hundred people, one family to a cottage, with the single men and boys divided among the families.

The small cottages were post-and-beam frame constructions

84

Thatching a roof *(reenactment photo)*

with thatched roofs, about twenty feet by twenty feet. The floors were dirt. The walls and chimneys were quickly built of wattle — a woven support of thin saplings — and daub — a stiff mixture of clay, sand, straw, and sometimes dung. For chimneys, the wattle and daub were built up around green hewn beams. The fireplaces were three to four feet deep and eight to ten feet long, a huge space in such a small house. And into some of these tiny, one-room houses, eight people moved.

The Leyden folk had seen desperate times before, but these early days in Plymouth were the most desperate of their lives. "But that which was most sadd and Lamentable," Bradford wrote, "was, that in 2. or 3. moneths time halfe of their company dyed, especially in January and February, being the depth of winter, and wanting houses and other comforts; being infected with the

scurvie and other diseases, which this long voyage and in-
acomodate condition had brought upon them." The sickness that
raged through January and February seems to have been a combination of scurvy, caused by the diet during the voyage; tuber-
culosis; and pneumonia, caused by the terrible exposure they had
endured. At its height, the sickness took two or three people a
day, so that by March the company was reduced to less than half
its original number.

At times there were only six or seven healthy colonists, who did
their best to help the others:

> To their great comendations be it spoken, [they] spared no pains,
> night nor day, but with abundance of toyle and hazard of their
> owne health, fetched them woode, made them fires, dressed them
> meat, made their beds, washed their loathsome cloaths, cloathed
> and uncloathed them; in a word, did all the homely and necessarie
> offices for them which dainty and queasy stomacks cannot endure
> to hear named; and all this willingly and cheerfully, without any
> grudging in the least, shewing herein their true love unto their
> friends and bretheren. A rare example and worthy to be remem-
> bered.

Of these rare examples, one was William Brewster — this
was to be expected. But the other is surprising. When one thinks
of Miles Standish, one does not think of the gentle and comfort-
ing hands of a nurse, but Bradford describes him in this way, and
perhaps this willingness to give so of himself cemented the
friendship between Bradford and Standish. "And yet the Lord so
upheld these persons, as in this generall calamity they were not at
all infected either with sicknes, or lameness . . . whilst they had
health, yea, or any strength continuing, they were not wanting to

any that had need of them. And I doubt not but their recompence is with the Lord."

The Pilgrims had built a storehouse along with the cottages — this to be set aside for supplies. Here, along with food and gunpowder, they now moved the sick. Joining them was Bradford, who had endured so much exposure during the three exploratory trips. On January 11 he was working out in one of the clearings when he was "vehemently taken with a grief and a pain, and so shot to his huckle-bone it was doubted that he would instantly have died." It is apparently the first time since his childhood illness that Bradford had been down with sickness, though his ankles had been troubling him since the third exploratory trip around Cape Cod. He was taken to the common house where he recovered some in the evening.

Three days later, however, he was still there when a spark ignited the thatched roof; the passengers still aboard the *Mayflower* must have thought the Indians had attacked. Sparks fell around kegs of gunpowder and charged muskets, but acting quickly, the Pilgrims saved the common house and all the sick, though there was great loss of clothing and property. Despite this setback, Bradford, "in time, through God's mercie in the use of means, recovered."

God's hand was much on Bradford's mind during these early days. When, during his illness, he asked a sailor for some beer, believing that water was one of the causes for the disease, the sailor refused to give it to him, since he was eager to preserve the beer for the journey home. The result among the sailors was dramatic: "the disease began to fall amongst them also, so as allmost halfe of their company dyed before they went away, and many of their officers and lustyest men." Captain Jones sent word to John Carver that the Pilgrims could have as much beer as they wanted.

On January 21 the entire company of the *Mayflower* came ashore for the first time, crowding together into the common house for the Sabbath services. But it would be two more months — four months since they first sighted the shore, eight months since they had left Leyden — before the Pilgrims were ready to receive them in their cottages. During these four months since sighting land, six had died in December; eight in January, including Rose Standish; seventeen in February; and thirteen in March. "Of a hundred persons," wrote Bradford, "scarce fifty remain, the living scarce able to bury the dead."

The toll of that first winter was terrible. Before spring, four entire families had been wiped out. Only three married couples remained; the others had lost one spouse. Of the wives, only five of eighteen remained. Of the nineteen heads of households, half were dead. Of the twenty-nine single men, nineteen were gone. The children did somewhat better, probably because their parents sacrificed themselves. None of the seven daughters died, and only three of the thirteen young boys — two of these were orphans who had come over as servants. Priscilla Mullins lost her entire family, parents and brother. John Goodman, who had left a bride in Leyden, was gone; William White died, leaving a wife to tend their baby and five-year-old son in this wilderness. In the end, it was a tiny group, with only a handful of men, that faced the task of securing a colony on the edge of a continent.

And it was a small group that was more than a little fearful. As the weeks went by, the Pilgrims became more and more concerned not that they had seen Indians, but that they had not. There seemed to be signs that there were some around; many "came skulking about them," but there was no contact. Yet there were the cleared cornfields, the smoke of distant fires, the very brief contacts that suggested a near presence.

Samoset, the first Indian that the Pilgrims met

In late January, Captain Jones saw two Indians on Clark's Island, watching the *Mayflower* until it was clear that they had been discovered. In mid-February, one of the Pilgrims saw twelve Indians marching toward Plymouth. When he gave the alarm, those working in the woods dropped their tools and rushed back to the buildings; when they returned, the tools were gone.

And then, finally, physical contact was made on March 16, when "a certain Indian came bouldly amongst them" — in fact, he came right to the common house and would have entered a meeting if the sentries had not stopped him — "and spoke to them in broken

English, which they could well understand, but marvelled at it." Bradford saw this entrance as astonishing, but providential. The name of the certain Indian was Samoset, and he came from Pemaquid Point in Maine. Having talked with English sea captains up and down the Newfoundland coast, he had learned their language and now used it to explain to the Pilgrims how the Pawtuxets in this area had been wiped out — a mystery that had worried the Pilgrims for some time.

He spoke with them well into the night. "He became profitable to them in acquainting them with many things concerning the state of the country in the east-parts wher he lived, which was afterwards profitable unto them; as also of the people hear, of their names, number, and strength; of their situation and distance from this place, and who was cheefe amongst them." All of this was information that Bradford would have appreciated, as it told the Pilgrims about the tribes with which they would have to deal. Any knowledge was helpful, he knew, especially when dealing from a position of weakness. Samoset also told the Pilgrims of Massasoit, who was the chief of the Wampanoag tribe and lived at Narragansett Bay, some forty miles south of Plymouth.

The Pilgrims were grateful for the information, but not sure quite what to do with Samoset. Upon coming he had asked for English beer, but they had none and gave "strong water" instead, probably brandy. They threw a bright red horseman's coat about him, since he was naked except for a leather thong. But now, at night, he refused to leave, and the Pilgrims set a guard to watch this savage who had come out from the woods.

In the morning the Pilgrims sent Samoset away with gifts, asking that he bring back others of the Wampanoag tribe. Perhaps the Pilgrims simply wanted to be rid of Samoset for a time so that they could digest this new information; if so, they might have been surprised when Samoset returned the next day with five members of a tribe they had thought was forty miles distant. It was the Sabbath, but the Indians had no sense of that when, after eating, they began to dance and sing to entertain the Pilgrims, not knowing that the Pilgrims thought this a dreadful sin. But perhaps the Pilgrims softened some when at the end of the dance the Indians produced all the tools that had been taken in February, as well as several beaver pelts to trade.

But it was still the Sabbath, so the Pilgrims would not trade. They told the Indians to come back again with more pelts, and they "would trucke for all." The five left, but Samoset remained behind, Bradford noting that he "either was sicke, or feigned himselfe so." When four days had passed and the five had not returned, the Pilgrims sent Samoset out after them, laden with his English gifts: a pair of shoes and stockings, as well as a shirt and hat and a piece of cloth to tie around his waist. None of these gifts were cheap in a colony cut off from supplies in England. As soon as he left, Miles Standish rushed to The Mount to add to the fortifications.

Samoset's return would forever change the lives of the Pilgrims at Plymouth. First, he brought not the five Indians who had come before, but news that Massasoit himself would soon be there, along with his brother Quadequina and most of their men. Bradford knew that this was a crucial moment in the colony's history; if this meeting did not lead to good relations, the Pilgrims would always have to be on their guard. And with such a small group left, they would probably be wiped out easily. This fear seemed to be confirmed when Massasoit presently arrived, "a very lustie man in his best years," accompanied by sixty braves. Even that small a force was triple what the Pilgrims could hope to mount.

Massasoit asked the Pilgrim leaders to cross Town Brook and meet; they would not. Instead, they asked Massasoit to come to them; he would not. In this dangerous moment, Edward Winslow left the side of his ill wife — she was to die in just a few days — and crossed the brook, carrying with him gifts of knives, a copper pot, a chain with a jewel, biscuits and butter, and "withall a Pot of strong water." What Massasoit was most taken with, however, was Winslow's sword and armor, but Winslow, always a diplomat, was able to put him off. In the end, it was decided that Winslow would remain with Quadequina while Massasoit went into Plymouth.

Once there, Miles Standish fell in behind him. They must have seemed an odd pair, Standish being much shorter than Massasoit. Massasoit came with twenty of his men, and all had their faces painted and their bodies decorated. They wore deerskins over their shoulders, and knives and tobacco pouches around their necks. The Pilgrims were determined to impress; after Massasoit was seated in the common house, there was a loud drumroll and John Carver entered. Massasoit rose and kissed the governor's hand, and Carver returned the favor; Bradford noted that Massasoit "looked greasily." They drank to each other, and then sat down and negotiated one of the longest lasting, best-kept peace treaties ever instituted in North America. It lasted for Massasoit's lifetime and was never seriously strained. Though it could not be the kind of "combination" that the Mayflower Compact had been, since these were two separate peoples, still it was the kind of peace that could be established between peoples who hold a mutual respect.

The Pilgrims and the Wampanoags promised that neither side "should injurie or doe hurte" to the other. If a Pilgrim hurt an Indian, he would be sent for punishment to the Indians; if an Indian hurt a Pilgrim, he would be sent for punishment to Plymouth. Neither side would steal from the other; any theft would have to be restored. And if another group warred against either side, the other side would come to their aid as allies. For forty years this would hold.

Massasoit arriving in Plymouth with his warriors

When Samoset had returned with the news of Massasoit's arrival, he had also brought with him another Indian: Squanto, who spoke English even better than Samoset did. Squanto had reputedly led a most extraordinary life. He had been captured from Cape Cod in 1614 by Captain Thomas Hunt, who brought him back to Europe and sold him to Spanish friars. Escaping from them, Squanto traveled to England, where he lived as a servant to John Slanie, treasurer of the Newfoundland Company. He probably sailed back to his homeland in one of Slanie's ships, only to find that his entire tribe had died or been scattered. He was the last of the Pawtuxets.

Squanto would become a virtual member of the colony, embracing its faith as well. It can truly be said that without Squanto, the Pilgrims would not have survived. Bradford became his closest friend, with strong bonds cementing their relationship. Both had lost their old homes; both had traded for new lives; both had led lives heaped with loss and sorrow. Bradford saw in Squanto one more sign of God's special blessing for these Pilgrims. "Squanto continued with them," Bradford later wrote, "and was their interpreter, and was a special instrument sent of God for their good beyond their expectation. He directed them how to set their corne, where to take fish, and to procure other comodities, and was also their pilott to bring them to unknowne places for their profitt, and never left them till he died."

With the coming of Squanto came the coming of spring, literally and figuratively. Friendly relations having been established, Wampanoags began to come into Plymouth frequently, often with wives and children, and always hungry, it seemed. Edward Winslow and Stephen Hopkins went to Massasoit to ask that not so many come around, since their supplies were limited. However, they would be welcome if they brought pelts to trade. (The Pilgrims had finally concluded that they would not pay off their debt with fishing, but with trading for furs.)

Spring also meant relief from the terrible sickness that had been with the Pilgrims since they landed. Bradford remembered that with spring, "it pleased God the mortalitie begane to cease amongst them, and the sick and lame recovered apace, which put as it were new life into them; though they had borne their sadd affliction with much patience and contentedness, as I thinke any people could do. But it was the Lord which upheld them, and had beforehand prepared them; many having long borne the yoake, yea from their youth." Bradford himself could attest to this. If all their perse-

...troubles might have made them physically weaker, cer- ...onger.

...ve-taking of the *Mayflower*; the ...gain. On April 5, 1621, she set ...Carver had held her there all ...ge from the Indians, should the ...also the Pilgrims' only alternate ...common house had shown that ...gone with a simple spark. But in ...ho once had been so eager to put ...their way, were for some time ...their men being dead, and of ...many lay sick and weake, the ...his men begine to recover, and the hait oi ....er sailors and fewer supplies, but at least he would not be troubled by the winter storms. As the *Mayflower* lifted anchor, Bradford must have watched from the shore and felt a final severing.

But spring also brought planting time, and here Squanto was pivotal. Of the seeds which the Pilgrims had brought, many did not sprout. So they turned to planting the seed corn they had found, and Squanto showed "them both the manner how to set it, and after how to dress and tend it." But it was not enough to merely plant; the corn needed fertilizer — and there was a ready supply: the fish. He showed them how to make netted traps, "all which they found true by triall and experience." The fish caught in the Town Brook were alewives, which are still found along the New England coast. Squanto showed the Pilgrims how to plant three of them in each corn hill, placing four kernels above them. He also taught them that they had to guard the corn against wolves until the fish had rotted away. It was the first of his many vital services.

Squanto saved the lives of the Pilgrims. Among other things, he showed them how to plant corn using fish for fertilizer. *(reenactment photo)*

Squanto showed the Pilgrims the abundance of food that lay about them, so that by the fall of 1621, Edward Winslow could write back to friends in England to describe a land that seemed to flow with milk and honey:

For fish and fowl we have great abundance; fresh cod in the summer is but coarse meat with us; our bay is full of lobsters all the summer and affordeth variety of other fish; in September we can take a hogs head of eels in a night, with small labor, and can dig them out of their beds all the winter. We have mussels . . . at our doors. Oyster we have none near, but we can have them brought by the Indians when we will; all the spring-time the earth sendeth forth naturally very good sallet herbs. Here are grapes, white and red, and very sweet and strong also. Strawberries, gooseberries, raspas, etc. Plums of three sorts, with black and red, being almost as good as a damson; abundance of roses, white, red, and damask, single, but very sweet indeed.

Winslow made it sound as though food were simply all around, merely for the plucking.

But not all was so hopeful in this first spring. "In this month of Aprill whilst they were bussie about their seed, their Governor (Mr. John Carver) came out of the field very sick, it being a hott day; he complained greatly of his head, and lay downe, and within a few howers his sences failed, so as he never spake more till he died, which was within a few days after. Whoss death was much lamented, and caused great heaviness amongst them, as there was cause."

They buried their first governor, shooting volleys over his grave. He was mourned by both the Saints and the Strangers as the evenhanded man who had kept the colony together, listening to all, a wise, gentle patriarch of sixty. His wife, Catherine, bereft, died five or six weeks later.

Needing a new leader, the Pilgrims turned not to another patriarch, and not to a leader of the church. They turned to William Bradford, who, at age thirty-two, stepped into the position of governor of Plymouth Colony. He would remain in that position for most of the rest of his life.

SIX

"Peace and Acquaintance"

"Shortly after William Bradford was chosen Governor in [John Carver's] stead, and being not yet recovered of his ilnes, in which he had been near the point of death, Isaak Allerton was chosen to be an Asistante unto him, who, by renewed election every year, continued sundry years togeather, which I hear note once for all." So does Bradford record the moment in his life when he stepped from being the farmer to being the governor, when he ceased being the young disciple and instead took on the leadership of the colony. William Brewster must have watched and remembered back to those early walks around Austerfield and Scrooby, when Bradford had been just a boy.

Now Bradford took his place among peers, as those who had governed the group — men like Brewster and John Robinson — became more like elder statesmen whose word was revered but who played less and less a role in the daily operations of the colony. Brewster in many ways was the leading church official, but Bradford was now the leading civic authority, and Miles Standish — not even a member of the church — was, at thirty-six, the leading military man. Bradford's assistant, Isaac Allerton, was only thirty-four, and Edward Winslow, who would later become a governor but was now used on diplomatic errands — like the one he had performed at Town Brook with Massasoit — was only twenty-six. All of these younger men had lost their wives, and perhaps the enormous energy they put into running the colony was a way for them to deal with their grief and loneliness.

Bradford and those he gathered around him brought to the Pilgrims a decisiveness and sense of prompt action that had never before marked them. Partly this decisiveness was necessary if the colony was to adapt and survive in a wilderness, but partly it came about because of Bradford's confidence that the Lord had led him to this point and would use him to establish a Christian commonwealth. It would be a commonwealth where all things would be guided by principles from the Scriptures, but the governance of the colony and the governance of the church would remain separate. Pastors would not rule, as they did in the Massachusetts Bay Colony that would be planted north of Plymouth. Any powers that the Scriptures did not specifically give to the church were, in Bradford's mind, reserved for the civil governor.

It was an entirely new vision for a way of life, and quite different from King James's view of himself as head of the Church of England. This Pilgrim vision would survive and prosper, even long after Plymouth Colony was gobbled up by the Massachusetts Bay Colony.

On May 12, 1621, as the planting was under way, Bradford performed a civil ceremony that suggested this sense of separation between the religious and civil spheres. Since marriage was not a duty given over to the church in the Scriptures, Bradford and the Pilgrims agreed that it was "a civill thing, upon which many questions aboute inheritances doe depende, with other things most proper to their cognizans . . . and no wher found in the gospell to be layed on the ministers as a part of their office." The wedding, nonetheless, must have been a moving one for Bradford. Edward Winslow, who had lost his wife seven weeks earlier, was marrying Susanna White, who had lost her husband. Bradford must have thought of Dorothy, who had spent time with Susanna's son, Resolved, during their journey to the New World. In seeing Susanna wed again, perhaps Bradford felt his own lonely situation even more keenly.

But even in his loneliness, Bradford the governor had enormous duties: there was still peace to establish firmly among the Indians; Massasoit was only one sachem among the chiefs of tribes all along Cape Cod. Peace with the Indians became especially important toward the end of May when young John Billington wandered away from the colony and got lost, ending up five days later twenty miles from Plymouth on an Indian plantation, from which he was taken to the very Indians the Pilgrims had fought on Cape Cod.

Bradford sent a message to Massasoit to see if he could help, and eventually Massasoit did find Billington and sent word to Plymouth. Bradford dispatched the shallop for him, and he came back with a number of men from the tribes the Pilgrims had so offended when they first landed. Bradford's sense of his role as governor was just in this case; he knew the Pilgrims had earlier been in the wrong. And so, the Pilgrims "gave full satisfaction to those whose corne they had found and taken when they were at Cap-Codd. Thus ther peace and acquaintance was prety well established with the natives about them." In this, Bradford's first action with the Indians as governor, he showed considerable skill and foresight.

Spring turned to summer, and the Pilgrims' colony began to prosper. There was much to learn about this New World, and Squanto was a willing teacher. He had remained in Plymouth, and probably was living in Bradford's house. In addition to the planting, he taught the Pilgrims how to find eels and trap deer, using the same kind of device for the latter that had tripped up Bradford when they first arrived. He showed them how to net birds, how to grind corn into "nocake," how to find certain berries in the woods. He taught them how to hunt bear, raccoons, otters, beavers, and muskrats. He showed them how to fish in the open bay and along the coast during the summer, and how to cut holes in the ice during the winter to catch pike, perch, and bream.

Still, many necessities were not immediately available, and when Edward Winslow wrote back to England with advice on what a colonist ought to bring, it was clear that these were much on his mind.

> Be careful to have a very good bread-room to put your biscuits in. Let your cask for beer and water be iron-bound for the first tier if not more. . . . Let your meal be so hard trod in your cask that you shall need an adze or hatchet to work it out with. . . . [B]ring good store of clothes and bedding with you. Bring every man a musket or fowling-piece; let your piece be long in the barrel; and fear not the weight of it, for most of our shooting is from stands. Bring juice of lemons, and take it fasting. . . . If you bring any thing for comfort in the country, butter or sallet oil, or both is very good. Our Indian corn, even the coarsest, maketh as pleasant meat as rice, therefore spare that unless to spend by the way; bring paper and linseed oil for your windows, with cotton oil for your lamps. Let your shot be most for big fowls, and bring store of powder and shot.

Most of these supplies concern food: the meal, the biscuits, the butter and oil, the fowling pieces and shot for larger game — which the colonists were never skilled at trapping.

102

Some of the Pilgrims' few — and precious — possessions

Top: Elder Brewster's chair and the cradle of Peregrine White

Middle: Sword, pot, and platter of Miles Standish

Lower: Ancient spinning wheel and Governor Carver's chair

Pilgrims trading for pelts with the Indians *(reenactment photo)*

Bradford had to see to the trading of the colony as well; they still had the entire debt to the Merchant Adventurers to pay off. Having for the most part given up the idea of fishing, the Pilgrims turned to trading for pelts. And these were plentiful. The Indians used a spring trap to capture deer, moose, wildcats, foxes, and even bears. Otters and beavers could chew out of these, so they used another kind which the colonists never seemed to learn how to use. As one early traveler to New England described it, "these beast are too cunning for the English, who seldom or never catch any of them." This trade also prospered.

As summer wore on, Plymouth began to look more like a town than a refugee camp. Twenty-six acres had been cleared. The road from the harbor to The Mount had seven finished houses on it, and more were under construction; after the sickness of the first winter, the Pilgrims no longer needed the nineteen houses they had origi-nally planned. Corn was ripening well, with ears bigger than the Pil-grims had ever grown in England, and the harvest looked to be good. On The Mount, cannon had been situated under Standish's watchful eye. Bradford had reason to be hopeful.

And he had yet another friend, Hobomok, one of the close counselors of Massasoit. Like Squanto, Hobomok came "to live amongst them, a proper lustie man, and a man of accounte for his vallour and parts amongst the Indeans, and continued very faithfull and constant to the English till he died." Both Hobomok and Squanto would continue to live at Plymouth, and were frequently jealous of each other.

In the middle of the summer came another test of Bradford's skill as governor. Hobomok and Squanto had gone to meet with a sachem named Corbitant in Namassakett, about fourteen miles west of Plymouth. Corbitant was an ally of Massasoit, but during the meet-ing a quarrel developed and Corbitant threatened to stab both Squanto and Hobomok. Hobomok fled back to Plymouth, where he told Bradford that Squanto had probably been killed "for no other cause but because they were friends to the English."

There was no indecision in Bradford; he recognized the threat: "for if they should suffer their freinds and messengers thus to be wronged, they should have none would cleave unto them, or give them any inteligence, or doe them serviss afterwards; but nexte they would fall upon them selves." He gathered together fourteen men under the command of Miles Standish, and with Hobomok as their guide, went back to the house in which Squanto had apparently per-ished.

Standish set the guard around the house and entered, commanding none to leave. When three tried, Pilgrim muskets wounded them. Neither Corbitant nor Squanto was there, but the Pilgrims learned that Squanto had only been threatened, not hurt. In fact, he appeared soon after, but not until the Indians who were with Corbitant came with provisions to offer for peace.

The accounts do not say whether Bradford was among the fourteen, but the generous response of the Pilgrims suggests he was: they brought the three wounded men back to Plymouth to dress their wounds. Bradford saw the event as having a good outcome: "After this they had many gratulations from diverse sachems, and much firmer peace." Even Corbitant, in the face of this action, sent messages through Massasoit that he would "make his peace."

Bradford felt that the colony was safer now than it had ever been, and that the colonists should be about the business of trading for more pelts to pay off the debt. On September 18 he sent the shallop north to Massachusetts Bay with Miles Standish in charge and Squanto as guide. Never known as a fine diplomat, Standish was able to befriend the Massachusett tribe and to trade for beaver pelts. The group returned with fine reports of the coast to the north, and perhaps for a moment — or longer — Bradford might have wished that they had settled in a better place. But they were settled here now, and the Lord had brought them to this place that now had so much of their blood in it. And besides, the Lord, Bradford later wrote, had appointed that other place for other uses; it is God "who assignes to all men the bounds of their habitations." If Plymouth had been appointed for the Pilgrims, then their only response should be one of thankfulness for the Lord's blessing. "[T]hey found the Lord to be with them in all their ways," he wrote, "and to blesse their outgoings and incommings, for which let his holy name have the praise forever, to all posterity."

Miles Standish leading an expedition with Squanto as guide

Fall came in, with the first chilling breezes from off the water. The leaves on the oaks started to brown, while the maples rushed to rioting colors. The Pilgrims remembered their first winter and its toll, but, taking stock, they found that God's blessing had brought them a kind of plenty they had never had before.

> They began now to gather in the small harvest they had, and to fitte up their houses and dwellings against winter, being all well recovered in health and strength, and had all things in good plenty; for as some were thus employed in affairs abroad, others were exersised in fishing, aboute codd, and bass, and other fish, of which they tooke good store, of which every family had their portion. All the sommer ther was no wante. And now began to come in store of foule, as winter aproached, of which this place did abound. . . . And besids water foule, ther was great store of wild Turkies, of which they tooke many, besids venison, etc. Besids they had aboute a peck a meale a weeke to a person, or now since harvest, Indean corne to that proportion.

The first American Thanksgiving

It must have given Bradford a pleasure unlike any other to see the stores brought in. If he had lost his wife, he had put all of his energies into husbanding the resources of Plymouth Colony.

With the fall came the harvest, and it seemed full. Though the six acres of English barley and peas were only "indifferent good," the twenty acres of corn sprouted and tasseled. Bradford was pleased; it seemed they would enter the winter well provisioned, and certainly with better shelter than they had had the previous winter. Remembering the habit of the Dutch, who celebrated their freedom from the Spanish with a holiday every October, Bradford decreed a day to be set aside so that all the Pilgrims might "after a more special manner, rejoyce together."

Fowl were gathered in, including "wild Turkies." Shellfish, eels, and lobsters were harvested from the tidal pools. There was corn bread to make, goose and duck to cook, leeks and watercress to be gathered, dried berries to be prepared. If this had been just for the fifty Pilgrims, the task might not have been so great. But to cement ties of friendship, Bradford sent Squanto to invite Massasoit, and when the sachem arrived on a beautiful October day, he brought with him ninety of his men, tripling the size of the company. Though the Pilgrims had prepared enough meat to feed the colony for an entire week, they had never thought to provide food for so many. Perhaps Massasoit understood; he sent five of his men back into the woods, and soon they returned with five deer.

Thus began three days of feasting. One hundred forty-two sat down to trestle tables, including the ten women who, with children and a handful of servants, prepared all the food. It was a grueling three days for them. Between meals the men played games of skill, and Massasoit was surprised to see that the Pilgrims' games were not so different from those his own people played. Bradford's invitation had been astute; it did cement a friendship.

But the harvest feast was more than that for the Pilgrims. It was a celebration of God's blessing. They had survived; they were even beginning to flourish. They sensed that God was with them. Edward Winslow, remembering that day two months later, wrote in a letter back to England that "although it be not always so plentiful as it was at this time with us, yet by the goodness of God, we are so far from want we often wish you partakers of our plenty."

In the next month, the Pilgrims began to prepare more thoroughly for the winter. Cracks in the houses were chinked, wood was brought in, and supplies were stored in the common house. But when Bradford inventoried the latter, he found to his disappointment that he had overestimated the size of the harvest. He believed that another ship from England was unlikely, and that he would have to cut the rations.

Bradford was right about the supplies, but wrong about the ship. On November 9, an Indian came running into Plymouth with news that a ship had been sighted off Cape Cod, evidently making for Plymouth. Here, perhaps, was a new enemy that the Pilgrims had not anticipated: Bradford imagined it might be a French ship sailing down from Canada, meaning to pillage the colony. Miles Standish rushed to The Mount to fire a warning cannon shot, and then made sure "every man, yea, boy, that could handle a gun was readie." But as the ship coasted into Plymouth harbor, she ran up an ensign with the red cross of England. Amazed, the Pilgrims put down their arms and crowded the beach. It was the *Fortune,* bringing with her thirty-five more of the Leyden congregation, including Robert Cushman.

Delighted, the Pilgrims crowded around for news of home. Edward Winslow's brother had come, as had Brewster's twenty-eight-year-old son Jonathan. But Bradford's son was not there, nor was their pastor, John Robinson. Of the thirty-five, there were only two women and a young girl, the Leyden congregation having judged that more men were needed.

If Bradford had hoped that more women would have joined the colony, he was disappointed. The passengers, however, were delighted, and not only for the reunion. When they had first sighted Cape Cod, they "saw nothing but a naked and barren place. They then begane to thinke what should become of them, if the people here were dead or cut off by the Indeans." Their fear grew so great that they considered stealing the sails from the ship so that it could not leave without them. But now, as they looked about them and saw the work that had been done that summer, all was different. "And they when they came a shore found all well, and saw plenty of vitails in every house, were no less glad."

The colonists rejoiced at the arrival of old friends and the addi-

The *Fortune* may have looked much like this seventeenth-century ship.

tion to their colony. But Bradford, thinking as a governor, saw that the arrival of the *Fortune* meant difficulties as well. He had already cut rations in half, yet here was almost a doubling of people to be fed. He hoped that the ship would have come fully provisioned, but this was not to be. "Ther was not so much as bisket-cake or any other victialls for them, neither had they any beding, but some sory things they had in their cabins, nor pot, nor pan, to drese any meate in; nor over many cloaths, for many of them had brusht away their coats and cloaks at Plimoth as they came." The plantation was glad of this addition of strength, but "could have wished that many of them had been of beter condition, and all of them beter furnished with provisions; but that could not now be helpte."

Robert Cushman was not to stay; he would return with the *Fortune*. This meant that Bradford had to find a way to divide thirty-four newcomers among the seven houses. (He probably wished they had completed the nineteen homes they had originally planned.) It is likely he had the common house converted into a dormitory of some sort, but even so, at least three or four new people would have had to go into each of the already overcrowded houses. Soon after the *Fortune* left, Bradford did indeed cut the rations.

But perhaps even more disappointing for Bradford was a letter sent from Weston, the man who had first gathered together the Merchant Adventurers. It was full, Bradford writes, of "complaints & expostulations." Weston demanded that they sign the original agreement that he had brokered with the Merchant Adventurers. He complained that they had kept the *Mayflower* too long, and that they should have sent it back filled with furs and clapboard and other goods to be used to pay off the debt. This can only have happened, he claimed, because of the Pilgrims' weakness of judgment, not weakness of hands. If they had spent only a quarter of the time they used for discoursing and arguing, they would have been able to do much more. He concluded the letter with the threat that the other Merchant Adventurers might quite soon withdraw their support.

It was a difficult letter to receive from someone sitting so comfortably in London. Bradford must have been tempted to return a bitter reply. But he knew that the colony was obligated to these Adventurers, even though they had sent no supplies for a year now. So Bradford directed that the *Fortune* be laden with goods that could be sold by the Adventurers. The Pilgrims stored her hold with beaver and other animal pelts for which they had traded with Massasoit. They added hardwood timber, wainscoting, and clapboard; it was a cargo that would pay off half of their debt.

But Bradford sent more than goods. He sent a very optimistic account of the colony that he and Edward Winslow had written, today known as *Mourt's Relation.* It would be published the next year in London. He sent a plea to the Adventurers, noting that the coming of the new group "would bring famine upon them unavoydably, if they had not supply in time." And he sent back a carefully worded note, answering the charges that Weston had brought against them.

> You greatly blame us for keping the ship so long in the countrie, and then to send her away emptie. She lay 5. weeks at Cap-Codd, whilst with many a weary step (after a long journey) and the indurance of many a hard brunte, we sought out in the foule winter a place of habitation. Then we went in so tedious a time to make provision of sheelter us and our goods, aboute which labour, many of our armes and leggs can tell us to this day we were not necligent. But it pleased God to vissite us then, with death dayly, and with so generall a disease, that the living were scarce able to burie the dead; and the well not in any measure sufficiente to tend the sick. And now to be so greatly blamed, for not fraighting the ship, doth indeed goe near us, and much discourage us.

The colony's hardship was probably underscored by the fact that Weston had addressed his letter to Governor Carver, but he had died months earlier.

The letter suggests Bradford's balanced approach to his role. He would answer charges forthrightly and even aggressively, but he would also have the ship provisioned so that the Adventurers would be satisfied. This balance marked all of his judgments and helped to forge the close ties among the colonists, who recognized that in Bradford they had a fair and tolerant man.

After two weeks the *Fortune* sailed away, and the colonists were once again alone. They did not know, as the *Fortune* sailed out of the harbor, that it would be captured by the French, who would take everything from it. All their hard work was for nothing.

But Bradford would soon be taken up with a more urgent problem than the Merchant Adventurers. Almost as soon as the *Fortune* had left, a Narragansett man walked defiantly into the colony and threw down a bundle of arrows tied together with a snakeskin, a message from the sachem Canonicus. Bradford did not know what to make of it, but both Squanto and Hobomok agreed that it was a challenge and an insult. Bradford knew that the Narragansetts could gather together hundreds of warriors; he could gather about fifty or so. But any sign of weakness, he felt, would mean disaster.

He had the snakeskin stuffed with bullets and sent back to the Narragansetts with a message: "If they had rather have warre then peace, they might begine when they would; they had done them no wrong, neither did they fear them, or should they find them unprovided." The Narragansetts refused to even touch the snakeskin, but had it sent back. They did not attack.

Bradford, however, recognized that despite their friendship with Massasoit, the Pilgrims were not safe from Indian attacks. In fact, it might have been that friendship that led the Narragansetts, who had ambitions over Massasoit's people, to see the Pilgrims as enemies. Bradford divided the men into squads of four; they developed strategies for defense, signals for alarms, and plans for putting out fires. Together with Miles Standish, Bradford decided that the town needed greater protection, and they resolved to build a mile-long log palisade around it. It would be a tremendous undertaking.

But before the work began, Bradford's authority would be chal-

The messenger of the Naragansett chief delivers a threat to Bradford.

lenged. On Christmas Day, 1621, Bradford called the colonists to work, as Christmas was not a holiday for the Separatists. But it was a holiday for the Strangers, and they grumbled that it went against their consciences to work on this day. Bradford must have sensed that allowing some a holiday while asking others to work would have caused some grumbling among the workers. But he also believed that the Strangers were indeed speaking out of a matter of conscience. "So the Governor told them that if they made it a matter of conscience, he would spare them till they were better informed." But when he came home at noon, Bradford found the Strangers at play, "some pitching the barr and some at stoole-ball, and shuch like sports. So he went to them, and tooke away their implements, and tould them that was against his conscience, that they should play and others worke." Let them keep to their houses, he

A squad of men in a gun drill, training to improve the defenses of the colony
(reenactment photo)

told them, and celebrate as a matter of devotion. "Since that time nothing hath been attempted that way, at least openly."

They began the palisade in February and finished it in the middle of March; it enclosed all of the houses and much of The Mount, and gave the colony more security than it had ever had. But until then, a guard needed to be kept, the squads drilled, and rations allotted to get them through the cold months. And there was always, in the back of Bradford's mind, the question of paying off the Merchant Adventurers. He began to make plans for a spring visit to the Massachusett tribe to trade for more beaver pelts.

Bradford had become the decisive governor the colony needed. Relying upon Scripture and the counsel of men like Miles Standish and William Brewster, he guided the colony through all the challenges that had so far faced it. There would be more; one of them would come sooner than he had imagined. But that, too, would be faced.

If Bradford, in the crowded house in which he lived, felt the loneliness of the leader, as well as the loneliness of the widower, he gave no sign. Perhaps he was too busy to feel loneliness, never mind acknowledge it.

SEVEN

"The Orchard in Winter"

If there were times when Bradford looked about him and felt that Plymouth Colony was finally secure, there must have been many more times when he felt that it was not. To the north lay the French in Canada and Maine, with large colonies and heavy interest in the same furs that interested the Pilgrims. To the south, the Dutch along the Hudson River claimed more and more land. On Cape Cod, the Pamet and the Nauset tribes held an uneasy truce with the Pilgrims; the Narragansett tribe to the south and west held an even more uneasy truce. To the north, the Massachusetts could be openly hostile, though willing to trade.

Even relations with Massasoit were strained in the spring of 1622, and Bradford needed all of his diplomatic skills to avoid war. Bradford found that Squanto had decided that he would try to lord it over the other tribes and become even more important than Massasoit. He "sought his owne ends, and plaid his owne game, by putting the Indeans in fear, and drawing gifts from them to enrich

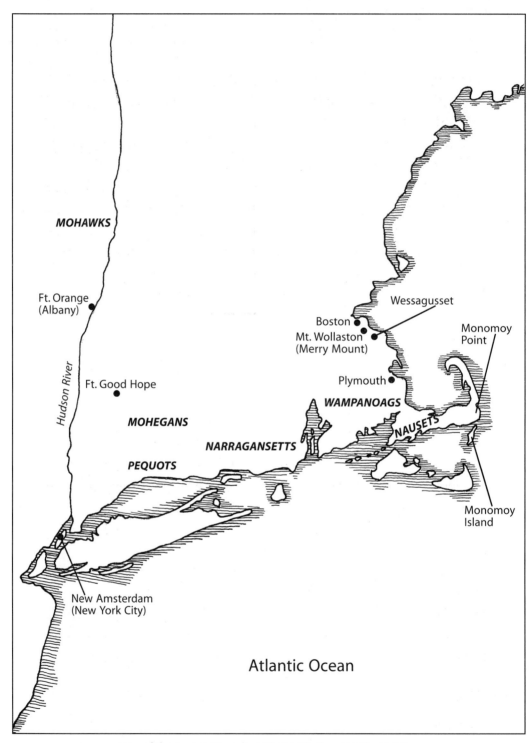

Map of the area surrounding Plymouth showing the location
of Indian tribes and other European settlements

him selfe; making them believe he could stur up warr against whom he would, & make peace for whom he would." Massasoit, hearing of this, sent a company to Plymouth with his own knife, a large present of beaver pelts, and the demand that the braves be allowed to take back Squanto's head and hands.

Bradford was always one to remember past friendships with grace and gratitude; he delayed. "It is not the manner of the English," he said, "to sell men's lives at a price, but when they have deserved justly to die, to give them their reward." He refused the gifts of the beaver pelts, though the colony certainly had need of them. When he sent for Squanto, the brave accused Hobomok of lying and told Bradford he would leave his fate to his decision.

It was a crucial moment for the colony: If Bradford did not hand over Squanto, he would be breaking the treaty with Massasoit. If he did, he would be breaking faith with himself. He looked about for a way out of this situation, and was saved when he saw a small boat out in Cape Cod Bay. Before he made such an important decision, he declared, he needed to know if this boat were a friend or an enemy. Massasoit's company, "mad with rage, and impatient at delay . . . departed in great heat." Bradford had saved the situation — for now.

But the coming of the boat showed another great weakness in the colony: the Pilgrims were slowly starving to death. The additional thirty-four colonists from the *Fortune* had strained their resources so thin that the colony would soon perish. This boat, the *Sparrow,* brought seven more settlers but no more supplies. It did bring letters from Weston, who wrote that these seven were not colonists and not under the Pilgrims' governance; they had come to set up a saltworks for Weston's own profit. The Pilgrims were to house and feed these men, to help them build what they would need, and to provide their seed corn. Failure to do so would be "extreme bar-

barism." In addition, more men were to follow who would set up another colony.

The Pilgrims themselves, wrote Weston, could expect no more support: "I find ye generall so backward and your friends in Leyden so cold that I fear you must stand on your own leggs and trust (as they say) to God and yourselves." Bradford had been doing this for a long time already, but it was hard to hear that there would be no supplies from England. And it was also hard to hear that there would soon be a rival colony close by, trading for the same pelts, competing, perhaps, for the same land. Perhaps even those who had come over on the *Fortune* were really destined not for Plymouth, but for this new colony. Suspicions grew.

All this was "but cold comfort to fill their hungrie bellies." Bradford was in such a quandary about this news that he decided not to share it with anyone but his most trusted counselors; he felt the news would bring the colony to absolute despair.

In late spring the number of fowl available for hunting decreased dramatically, and the Pilgrims faced even worse conditions than before. Edward Winslow noted that "Everything must be expected in its proper season. 'No man,' as one saith, 'will go into the orchard in winter, to gather cherries.'" With the birds gone, the Pilgrims turned to fishing, but they were inept. Cape Cod Bay was "full of bass and other fish, yet for want of fit and strong . . . netting, they, for the most part, brake through and carried all away before them. And though the sea were full of Cod, yet we had neither tackle nor hawsers for our shallops." Growing more and more concerned, Bradford dared not turn even to Massasoit for help, since the affair with Squanto was still not settled and he did not wish to show the colony's weakness.

By midsummer, two more of Weston's ships arrived, the *Charity* and the *Swan*. They carried sixty more men for the new colony;

they brought absolutely no supplies with them, not even, wrote Bradford, a "bite of bread." Weston asked Plymouth to house and feed this new group and to help them set up the new colony that would rival Plymouth, establishing it north toward Massachusetts Bay. If Bradford was angered by this presumption, he did not show it; his response was typically generous, and he was undoubtedly glad that he had continued to build new houses.

> All these things they pondred and well considered, yet concluded to give his men frendly entertainmente; partly in regard of Mr. Weston him selfe, considering what he had been unto them, and done for them, and to some, more espetially; and partly in compassion to the people, who were now come into a wilderness, (as them selves were,) and were by the ship to be presently put a shore (for she was to cary other passengers to Virginia, who lay at great charge,) and they were alltogeather unacquainted and knew not what to doe. So as they had received his former company of 7. men, and vitailed them as their owne hitherto, so they also received these (being about 60. lusty men), and gave housing for them selves and their goods; and many being sicke, they had the best meanes the place could aforde them.

Bradford's generous response was extraordinary; even as his own people were starving, he was willing to save those from a colony that might well be the end of Plymouth.

One letter from these three ships did bring some hope to Bradford, but it was not from Weston. Each spring and summer a fishing fleet came out from England and fished the waters off northern New England. One of the captains in that fleet, John Huddleston, sent word to the Pilgrims that three hundred of the colonists in Virginia had been massacred by the Indians and they should look to

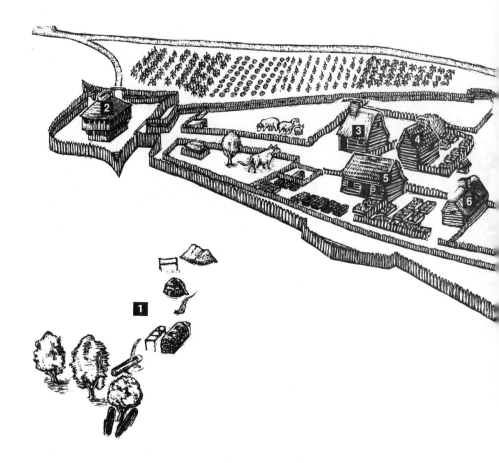

1. **Hobbamock's Homesite**
   Hobbamock, a counselor to Massasoit, came with his family to live in Plymouth in the spring of 1621 after a peace treaty with the colonists.

2. **The Fort/Meetinghouse**
   This "blockhouse" was built in 1622, primarily for defense. It was also used as a "meetinghouse," a place of worship, a courthouse, and a jail.

3. **Standish House**
   Veteran soldier Myles Standish, the military commander of New Plymouth, arrived on the *Mayflower*.

4. **Alden House**
   John Alden served as the cooper or barrelmaker aboard the *Mayflower*.

5. **Winslow House**
   Edward Winslow, a leading citizen of New Plymouth, came aboard the *Mayflower*.

6. **Cooke House**
   Francis Cooke arrived on the *Mayflower* with his son, John.

7. **Allerton House**
   Mayflower passenger Issac Allerton married Elder William Brewster's daughter, Fear.

8. **Bradford House**
   William Bradford succeeded John Carver as governor of the colony in the summer of 1621.

9. **Billington House**
   John Billington's family was one of the few to survive the terrible first winter unscathed by disease or accident.

10. **Brewster House**
    William Brewster was the religious leader, though not an ordained minister.

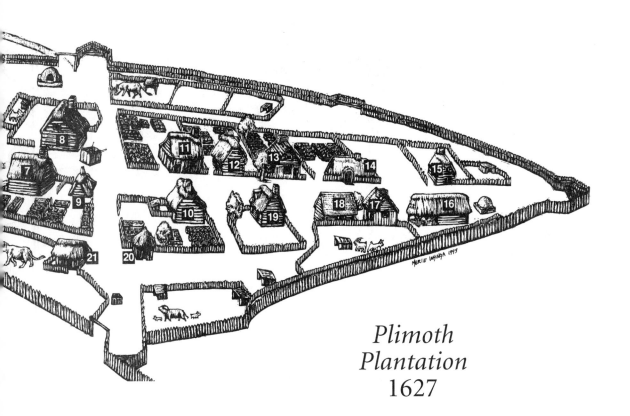

Plimoth
Plantation
1627

11. **Hopkins House**
Stephen Hopkins, a non-
separatist and businessman,
arrived with his family on
the *Mayflower*.

12. **Howland House**
John Howland was a servant
of the colony's first governor,
John Carver.

13. **Fuller House**
Samuel Fuller was a surgeon.
His wife Bridget was skilled
in midwifery.

14. **Annable House**
Anthony and Jane Annable
lived here with their two
daughters.

15. **Soule House**
George Soule came on the
Mayflower as a servant to
Edward Winslow and later
set up his own household.

16. **Storehouse**
Community supplies kept here.

17. **Common House**
This was the first structure built
in New Plymouth. It sheltered
some *Mayflower* passengers
until families were able to
build their own houses.

18. **Storehouse**
This outbuilding served
as a depot for furs and
other goods.

19. **Browne House**
Peter Browne was an un-
married man who came to
seek his fortune.

20. **Dutch Barn or Helm**
This is a hayhouse where
salt hay was stored.

21. **Cow House**
Cattle and farm animals were
housed in smaller "beast-
houses" such as this.

their defenses. "Hapie is he whom other mens harmes doth make to beware," he warned.

The tone of Huddleston's letter was so friendly, so intimate, that Bradford decided to take a risk. He sent Edward Winslow out in the shallop to find Huddleston and to see if he might trade provisions for furs. What Winslow found was perhaps more and less than he had hoped. He found "kinde entertainment and good respect, with a willingnesse to supply our wants." But Huddleston did not have as many supplies as were necessary, though he gave them as much as he could, enough, he said, to see them through to harvest time. Meanwhile the Pilgrims began to build a strong fort, despite their weakened condition. It was set with a flat roof and battlements, and cannon were mounted on top, where patrols watched through the day and night.

By the time Winslow returned with Huddleston's supplies, the colonists' situation was so desperate that Bradford had to keep the supplies locked up and guarded; "had it been in their owne custody, they would have eate it up and then starved." As it was, even with the additional supplies, Bradford could only raise the rations by a quarter of a pound of bread for each day.

Everyone waited for the corn to come in and for the end of their hunger. But when it did finally come in, "it arose but to a litle . . . partly by reason they were not yet well acquainted with the manner of Indean corne (and they had no other,) allso their many other imployments, but cheefly their weaknes for wante of food, to tend it as they should have done."

More disturbing, however, were the thefts. Even before the corn fully ripened, the colonists were driven by hunger to sneak into the fields and steal food to eat. "And though many were well whipt (when they were taken) for a few ears of corne, yet hunger made others (whom conscience did not restraine) to venture."

Harvesting rye at Plymouth. The fort can be seen in the background. *(reenactment photo)*

Bradford blamed the men that Weston had recently sent over for the thefts, and perhaps he was right in this. Robert Cushman had sent a letter warning Bradford that Weston's men were not to be trusted, and that it should be made plain to the Indians that they were a separate group, not part of Plymouth, since they were sure to make trouble later on. Bradford took this to heart and was undoubtedly pleased when in the early fall the sixty new colonists settled forty miles north in a place called Wessagusset, where they set up their own trading post.

Very soon, Weston's new colony began making overtures to Plymouth. With the harvest poor and winter upon them, both colonies recognized that they would have to explore for additional food.

Wessagusset proposed a joint venture: it would provide the *Swan*, which would take the Pilgrims' shallop in tow, to be used to transport supplies from the beach to the *Swan*. Bradford agreed, probably because he saw that the *Swan* could range much farther than the shallop. After several delays, Bradford himself set out in the ship in November, with Squanto as guide. It was, like so many of these voyages, a disappointing trip; it would bring little food and a terrible loss.

They rounded Cape Cod but were soon among the breakers that had so endangered the *Mayflower* not long before. Putting in at Monomoy, Bradford led a group ashore, Squanto among them, to see if there might be any trading. With Squanto's help, Bradford's group was welcomed, the Indians refreshing "them very well with store of venison and other victuals, which they brought them in great abundance, promising to trade with them." It was a good start; they traded for eight barrels of corn and beans.

But any joy that Bradford felt was tempered by sorrow. At Monomoy, "Squanto fell sick of an Indean fever, bleeding much at the nose (which the Indeans take for a symptom of death), and within a few days died ther; desiring the Governor to pray for him, that he might goe to the Englishmens God in heaven, and bequeathed sundrie of his things to sundry of his English freinds, as remembrances of his love; of whom they had a great loss." Bradford's sorrow was very real; his description of Squanto's death is much fuller than that of his own wife. He had been a true and close friend, and Bradford understood that Squanto was the key to the success of Plymouth Colony. Without him, the dream would have died.

But there was still Plymouth to feed. They left Monomoy and headed north to the Massachusetts, but there was no trade there. They sailed back south along the bottom of Cape Cod Bay, and at

Cummaquid traded for as many supplies as the Indians could provide. While these were being gathered, the Pilgrims sailed on to the Nausets, where they traded for ten more barrels of corn and beans.

But before these could be loaded, a storm struck the *Swan* and ripped the shallop away, dashing her against the beach. Without the shallop, they could not load the *Swan.* They left the corn covered with Indian mats, and Bradford made it known that they would come back for both the food and the shallop, and if either were touched, the thieves "should certainly smart for their unjust and dishonest dealing."

Bradford then led the other Pilgrims back by foot along the Cape Cod coast, stopping at Cummaquid to check on the food being gathered; the Wessagusset men sailed back to Plymouth to drop off four of the eight barrels of corn and beans. As soon as he returned to Plymouth, Bradford set off on another excursion — again on foot — to the inland villages, where he traded for additional corn. In all of this, Bradford wrote, the Indians gave them well more than they could spare, and Bradford's heart warmed to them. The corn would enable Plymouth to make it through the winter — just barely.

But relations were not so successful at Wessagusset. The colony's governor was not wise and able, as Bradford was, and the people ran through their stores much faster than they had imagined. They were soon selling blankets to the Indians, and even their clothes, and finally they began to steal from them, until the Indians demanded that one of them, a young man who had repeatedly stolen, be punished. The colonists at Wessagusset, who needed strong young backs, hung instead a guiltless old man.

Soon they had run out of all food, including their seed corn, and the Indians refused to trade with them. In fact, the Indians were suffering, too, and had nothing to spare, and no one at Wessagusset

A man doles out precious kernels of corn.
The cramped, one-room hut was typical of the Pilgrims' early homes.

had given them any reason to suffer for them. John Sanders, the governor of Wessagusset, refused to believe this; he felt that the Massachusetts were hoarding food, hoping that the English would starve. In February he sent a letter to Bradford, asking whether he might use force to take the food he wanted, since the Indians refused to trade. Bradford knew the Indians might not make much of a distinction between the two colonies, and he wrote back quickly: "We altogether dislike your intendment," which was "against the law of God and Nature." Sanders agreed, but word of his idea reached the Massachusetts, and there was talk of destroying the Wessagusset colony. In fact, some braves went down to tribes along Cape Cod to see if they might be willing to destroy Plymouth as well, lest those in Plymouth try to avenge their comrades.

Bradford must have sighed with the weariness of it all.

When it seemed as if things could not get much worse, they did: Bradford heard that Massasoit, the colony's closest Indian friend, was dying. Here was the one man who might have been able to stop the war against Plymouth. Bradford, needing to stay at the colony, quickly sent Edward Winslow to Massasoit. He found him in a crowded hut, filled with people who were "making such a hellish noise, as it distempered us that were well, and therefore unlike to ease him that was sicke."

Winslow found Massasoit in a terrible state, having already gone blind. He said: "Matta neen wonckanet namen, Winsnow" ("I shall never see you again, Winslow"). Winslow told him that Bradford had sent some medicines to help him, and, forcing open Massasoit's teeth with the point of his knife, Winslow got the sachem to swallow the first thing he had taken in two days. He scraped his tongue, taking away "abundance of corruption out of the same," and then sent for medicines and chickens from Plymouth. When the messenger went off, Winslow contrived a broth that Massasoit drank, and then he shot a duck and prepared it for the now-hungry chief.

Massasoit insisted on eating the fat, and within hours he had lost everything he had eaten and was bleeding at the nose — the same deadly symptom that Squanto had shown. He was sure he would soon die. But he rested, and by the time the chickens came from Plymouth he was feeling better and decided to keep them for breeding. (He later recovered his sight). He turned to Winslow and spoke the words he would tell to tribes all around Cape Cod: "Now I see the English are my friends and love me. And whilst I live, I will never forget this kindness they have showed me." He then told Winslow the names of the Indians who were conspiring against both Wessagusset and Plymouth, chief among them being a man named Wituwamat.

Statue of Massasoit

But Bradford was reluctant to wage war with tribes that had been so helpful; and after all, part of the reason for their colony was to bring the gospel to the Indians, not to kill them. On March 23, Bradford laid the case before the colony's annual meeting and asked for advice; the colony told Bradford that the situation and decision were completely in his hands — a sign of their confidence in him. Still reluctant, Bradford decided to send Miles Standish and several men to Wessagusset, there to end the conspiracy against the colonies by killing Wituwamat. In reaching this decision, Bradford balanced what he knew his pastor, John Robinson, would have said, with what he felt was in the best interest of the survival of the colony.

When Standish reached Wessagusset, he told John Sanders of his intentions; there must have been some bitterness here, because it was Sanders and his men that had caused the situation. The very next day they received what Standish called a threatening and insolent visit from Wituwamat himself, accompanied by a brave named Pecksuot. Pecksuot, who towered above Standish, chose to utter an unfortunate jibe at Standish: "Though you are a great captain, yet you are but a little man. Though I be no sachem, yet I am a man of strength and courage." He could hardly have chosen words that would infuriate Standish more.

The next day Pecksuot and Wituwamat returned, together with Wituwamat's eighteen-year-old brother and another man. Quietly Standish had the door barred, and then "began himself with Pecksuot, and snatching his own knife from his neck, though with much struggling, killed them [Pecksuot and Wituwamat's brother] therewith." The other brave was killed, as well as Wituwamat: "It is incredible," Winslow wrote, "how many wounds these two . . . received before they died, not making any fearful noise, but catching at their weapons and striving to the last." Standish returned to Plymouth with Wituwamat's head and was "received with joy, the head being brought to the fort and there set up."

But Bradford did not receive this with joy. Perhaps it reminded him of the excesses of Elizabeth and James, who set their enemies' heads on stakes. He felt that he had done this for the good of the colony, but the episode was painful to him. Like Dorothy's death, he chose not to include it in his *Of Plimoth Plantation*. And he probably nodded with agreement when he received a letter from John Robinson, who had heard of the slaughter in Leyden. "It is a thing more glorious in men's eyes than pleasing in God's, or conveniente for Christians, to be a terrour to poore barbarous people. . . . Oh! How happy a thing had it been, if you had converted some, before you had killed any." Bradford may have rationalized that this "poore barbarous people" had been preparing to wipe him out, but he must also have acknowledged the truth of Robinson's words.

Robinson also warned against Standish, though gently. "Upon this occasion let me be bold to exhorte you seriously to consider of the disposition of your Captaine, whom I love and am perswaded the Lord in great mercie and for much good hath sent you him, if you use him aright. He is a man humble and meek amongst you and towards all in ordinarie course. . . . But there may be wanting that tendernes of the life of man (made after God's image) which is meete." There is no record of Bradford rebuking Standish for what happened at Wessagusset; after all, Bradford had himself sent him to take Wituwamat's life. Actually the warning fell more on Bradford than it did upon Standish, and Bradford was to take it to heart.

Meanwhile, none of this had helped affairs at Wessagusset; the colony was still slowly starving. Bradford's tone is just a bit self-satisfied when he reasons about their distress: "It may be thought strange that these people should fall to these extremities in so short a time, being left competently provided [by the Plymouth colony] when the ship left them, and had an addition by that moiety of corn that was got by trade, besides much they gott of the Indians wher they lived, by one means and other. It must needs be their great disorder, for they spent excessively whilst they had, or could get it; and, it may be, wasted parte away among the Indeans." Perhaps this was not fair; Plymouth itself was not in much better condition.

Standish returned to Wessagusset and asked Sanders and his colonists what they wished to do; they could not remain there with no food, and it was unlikely that after this episode they would find Indians willing to trade with them. Standish offered to take the men back to Plymouth, but they had had enough. They decided to sail north to Maine in the *Swan,* there hoping to hear news of Thomas Weston. If they did not hear of him, they would take passage in the fishing ships and return to England. So ended the colony at

The first seal of Plymouth Colony, stamped "1620"

Wessagusset, and the Pilgrims were not sorry to see it go. Had the colony prospered, Bradford knew, it would have been a dangerous trading rival.

In the spring of 1623, Bradford was again elected governor; he had seen the colony through so many difficult times that the choice seemed obvious. As Bradford thought about facing yet another hungry summer, he was surprised when, in April, Thomas Weston himself arrived in the colony, stumbling in with little but his clothes. He had been shipwrecked north of Plymouth, and all that he had had been taken by the Indians. The one thing he did come laden with was promises: he "tould them he had hope of a ship and good supply to come to him, and then they should have any thing for it they stood in neede of." All they had to do was let him borrow some beaver pelts.

Bradford did not believe him; too many promises had been broken. And besides, "they had not much bever, and if they should let him have it, it were enoughe to make a mutinie among the people, seeing ther was no other means to procure them food which they so much wanted, and cloaths allso."

Nevertheless, Bradford, as before, remembered his early help. Secretly, Bradford and the other Pilgrim leaders loaned Weston about 170 pounds of pelts, which represented all the wealth that Weston now had. But when Weston was later retrieved by one of his men's ships, there was no repayment, and no supplies ever came from him. Bradford wrote that he became a bitter enemy to the Pilgrims, but "his malice could not prevaile."

Scarcely had Bradford finished with this problem and settled down to the next planting season when another ship put into Plymouth harbor, this with an altogether different challenge. It was the *Plantation,* under the command of Captain Thomas West, who had recently been named the admiral of New England by Ferdinando Gorges, a wealthy man who dreamed of an empire in New England. According to West, the Pilgrims would have to pay an enormous fee for a license to fish. They had no money or goods to comply with this demand, and besides, the outrage of such a proposition would have ensured Bradford's refusal in any case. When West saw that they would not pay, he also saw that the colony was starving. "Seeing their wants," he demanded extraordinary high fees for two barrels of dried peas. The barrels must have been very tempting, but Bradford said that, as "they had lived long without," they could continue to live without peas "rather than give so unreasonably."

But the *Plantation* left another, larger worry behind: At sea it had passed a ship bound for Plymouth and filled with passengers. West was surprised that she had not yet arrived, "fearing some miscarriage, for they lost her in a storme." This boat was the *Anne,* cramped with supplies and sixty passengers. He had also heard of the *Little James,* a ship that was intended to stay at Plymouth for the use of the Pilgrims, carrying another thirty passengers. Bradford knew that the ships West reported were probably carrying friends and family; they might also be carrying one Alice Southworth, whom he had known back in Leyden. He had written, begging her to come over. As the colonists carried on with their work, many an eye would have been trained out to sea.

But there was still the planting to think about, and in March, Bradford decided on a bold step. He had felt all along that one of the difficulties with their system of harvest was that everyone worked for "the general" good, rather than for his or her own family. Whether one worked hard or leisurely, whether one went early or late to the fields, the same amount of food was guaranteed that person. There was no private property, no incentive to work harder than anyone else, no chance to use individual talents to good effect. And all this came about because of the agreement with the Merchant Adventurers.

Bradford chose to break the agreement. He set aside a certain number of acres for each household in the colony; what they grew, they would keep. "This had very good success; for it made all hands very industrious, so as much more corne was planted then other waise would have bene by any means the Governor or any other could use, and saved him a great deall of trouble, and gave farr better contente."

From April through May the colonists planted their seed corn, dragging baskets full of alewives up the slopes to plant with the seeds. But as the corn was planted, so the supplies to eat dwindled. "All ther victails were spente, and they were only to rest on God's providence; at night not many times knowing wher to have a bitt of any thing the next day."

137

The large hearth was used for both heating and cooking in the Pilgrims' homes, but in the early years the cooking pots were often nearly empty.

Bradford organized the men into companies of six or seven and sent them to sea, so that as soon as one company returned, the next went out. The Pilgrims were not fishermen and were not quick at catching the cod that swam so abundantly in the bay, but they did not "return till they had caught something, though it were 5 or 6 days before, for they knew ther was nothing at home, and to go home emptie would be a great discouragemente to the rest."

With the spring the deer were on the move, and Bradford kept one or two hunters out in the woods each day. When a deer was caught, it was shared equally among all of the households. Knowing that there would be little chance of supplies from England, Bradford had done all he could as governor.

But by late May, Bradford saw there were some things he could not control. A drought blighted the harvest. According to Edward Winslow's account, the corn stalks sent out ears before the stalks were fully grown, and soon after the ears shriveled, the leaves browned, and the stalks died. "Our Beanes also ran not up according to their wonted manner, but stood at a stay, many being parched away, as though they had been scorched before the fire."

Bradford turned to God. By the end of July, he declared a "Day of Humiliation" when they would "humble themselves together before the Lord by fasting and prayer." On that hot day, the Pilgrims walked up to the fort on top of The Mount; Bradford, Standish, and Brewster came last. The entire day they spent praying, knowing that their loved ones were still at sea — and perhaps lost — and that the colony would not survive if the harvest did not prosper.

Their prayers were answered. "Before our departure," wrote Winslow, "the weather was over-cast, the clouds gathered together on all sides, and on the next morning distilled such soft, sweet, and moderate showers of rayne, continuing some fourteene dayes, and mised with such seasonable weather, as it was hard to say whether our withered Corne, or droupling affections were most quikned or revived. Such was the bountie and goodnes of our God."

But this was not the only prayer to be answered. Soon afterward, the *Anne* arrived; the *Little James* would follow in ten days. They brought with them ninety-three more colonists, one-third of them Saints, two-thirds Strangers. Across the bay came one Barbara, who would soon marry Miles Standish. The Brewsters' two daughters, Patience and Fear, arrived; Fear would soon marry Isaac Allerton. George Morton stepped onto shore as well, along with his wife, four children, nephew, and sister-in-law, Alice Southworth. Bradford must have been deeply moved.

But Bradford's son did not step ashore; he was still in Leyden. Perhaps he had found a new family that he had no wish to leave. He knew that his mother had died, and memories of his father would be faint. There was no incentive for him to leave his known world.

Those who had made the journey were aghast. "These passengers, when they saw their low and poore condition a shore, were much danted and dismayed, and according to their diverse humores were diversly affected; some wishing them selves in England againe; others fell a weeping, fancying their own miserie in what they saw now in others; other some pitying the distress they saw their friends had been long in, and still were under; in a word, all were full of sadnes. Only some of their old freinds rejoysed to see them, and it was no worse with them, for they could not expecte it should be better, and now hoped they should injoye better days togeather."

Bradford hoped for better days as well. He led Alice to his own home, situated behind a fence at the only crossroads in Plymouth, on the largest plot. No record exists as to what words passed between them, but it would not be long before they were married.

EIGHT

"Honor or Benefit"

William Bradford was approaching his thirty-fourth year; the last three of those had been spent as governor. In all that time he had never been far from a crisis. In all that time, he had been the one to whom the other Pilgrims turned first — not William Brewster or Miles Standish. His was the most public life in Plymouth; he worked side by side at the palisade, in the fields, by the harbor with all of the other colonists. It was a model of governing that was completely new to those used to an aristocracy.

With the coming of the new colonists, Bradford felt that he now had more than a toehold on the edge of the continent; Plymouth was more secure than it had ever been — at least in terms of the number of men who could be armed. It would never be a strong colony in terms of military strength, but Bradford was not interested in strength of that sort. He was only interested in strength as it served to keep the colony independent, free to follow the Separatist cause.

But the coming of the new colonists also called for Bradford's skills with compromise and negotiation. He was not altogether pleased with the newcomers; some were "very usefull persons," but others, especially among the Strangers, he thought were "so bad as they were faine . . . to send them home againe the next year." Perhaps Bradford felt this way because of the tension that quickly developed between the newcomers and what came to be called the "Old Comers" or "Old Planters," those who had come in the first four ships.

The new colonists recognized that it would be some time before they could become self-sufficient. They would therefore have to depend upon the supplies they brought, and they feared that the Old Comers wanted to use those supplies for themselves — which they did. The Old Comers, on the other hand, feared that their harvest was scanty at best, and that the newcomers would stretch their own supplies to an impossibly thin line. Bradford offered a compromise: the newcomers would use their own supplies until they were self-sufficient, and they would not claim any of the Old Comers' supplies at all. Both sides quickly agreed, and perhaps here Bradford's reputation as a fair, impartial judge was made with the newcomers.

As housing began to go up for the newcomers, Bradford watched over the harvest while directing goods and produce to the shoreline. There was still the Merchant Adventurers' debt to pay off, and he had the *Anne* stored with beaver pelts, clapboard, and wainscoting — the same sort of goods he had sent over before and lost to French raiders. Bradford also decided that Edward Winslow would return to England on the *Anne,* there to arrange with the Adventurers for additional, regular supplies. Bradford knew this would probably not be a successful mission, but as governor he would take all opportunities that came along.

Plymouth grew as it welcomed new colonists. *(reenactment photo)*

The prayer and care for the harvest that had seemed to be withering under the summer sun ended with joy. For the first time, the harvest was full and good, "and in stead of famine, now God gave them plentie, and the face of things was changed, to the rejoysing of the harts of many, for which they blessed God. And the effect of their particular planting was well seene, for all had, one way and other, pretty well to bring the year aboute, and some of the abler sorte and more industrious had to spare, and sell to others, so as any generall wante or famine hath not been amongst them since to this day." The Pilgrims had mastered the art of growing corn in New England, and they had planted more fields than ever before. But Bradford knew that his plan for dividing the acres into private lots had encouraged the Pilgrims to work harder than they might have otherwise. Altogether, he knew the harvest was the blessing of God.

But Bradford never seemed to have any long periods of rejoicing. Even as the harvest was readying, another ship put into harbor, this captained by Robert Gorges, son of Ferdinando Gorges, who was still trying to establish his New England empire. The Council for New England back in London had declared that Robert Gorges was "to be generall Governor of the cuntrie." Bradford was suddenly nothing but an assistant, and that for only a short time. Bradford did not mind losing the honor, but he suddenly feared that the governance of the colony would be taken out of the Pilgrims' hands, and how would they keep their Separatist ways alive then?

This fear grew even greater when Bradford met William Morrell, also on board with Gorges. He was an amateur poet — hardly a suitable occupation to help found a colony in the wilderness. But more worrisome was that he was an Anglican clergyman, wearing the vestments of the Church of England. He, Gorges declared, was to have "authority of superintendencie" over all churches in New England. Suddenly the Separatist Pilgrims felt they were back where they had started; they had traveled over an ocean, been exiled from their homes not once, but twice, and survived starvation and attack. Yet here, once again, was the Church of England to tell them how they must worship.

Gorges, Morrell, and the rest of Gorges's men stayed in Plymouth for two weeks, where Bradford, typically, had them "kindly entertained." Then Gorges sailed for Wessagusset, where he was to establish, presumably, his capital, and from which Morrell was to compel all the churches to follow the Church of England rule. But Gorges and Morrell had neither the vision nor the fortitude that sustained Bradford and the Pilgrims; they were not seeking out an entirely new way of living, but holding desperately on to the old in conditions that would not allow such holding. When Gorges saw Wessagusset and the work required to make it a viable colony, he

A wedding ceremony at Plymouth — more modest than the one that
united Bradford and Alice Southworth *(reenactment photo)*

"returned for England, haveing scarcely saluted the cuntrie in his
Governmente, not finding the state of things hear to answer his
quallitie and condition" — the last remark one that comes from
Bradford's yeoman past.

Some of Gorges's people also returned to England; some went
south to Virginia; and some remained at Plymouth, where they
"were helped with supplies." Morrell held on at Wessagusset for one
year, and though he had the authority to change the church worship, "he never shewed it, or made any use of it." The reason for this,
Bradford writes, is that he must have seen that such an attempt "was
in vaine." He returned to England, taking with him one benefit from
his year at Wessagusset: a long Latin poem about New England that
showed how impressed he was with its "ghusts of wind."

Amidst all this tension, Bradford and Alice Southworth married in high summer. It was not a religious ceremony, but it was certainly a public one, given that this was the governor who was to be married. Isaac Allerton, as deputy governor, performed the ceremony at the fort atop The Mount. With that ceremony Bradford became a stepfather to two young children, still not arrived in the colony. He and Alice would eventually have four of their own. Meanwhile Bradford's son, John, was still in Leyden or perhaps England, and there is no record that Bradford was eager for him to come to Plymouth. Perhaps he would have been a painful reminder of Dorothy and the terrible sadness of her death.

By the spring of 1624, Bradford had grown tired of his responsibilities. The colony was on a firm standing now, and he asked to be excused from the governorship, arguing that changing governors was a necessary move. "If it was any honour or benefite, it was fitte others should be made partakers of it; if it was a burthen, (as doubtles it was,) it was but equall others should help to bear it."

The colonists did not agree. Because Bradford had steered them through so many perilous courses already, he was best qualified to steer them through any new dangers — and there was no guarantee that there would be no new dangers. Bradford reluctantly agreed, asking that the number of his assistants be increased from one to five "for help and counsell, and the better carrying on of affairs." This number would eventually be increased to seven, where it remained for the rest of Bradford's governorship.

The governor's duties were extraordinary, and they must have seemed particularly pressing to a newly married man eager to begin a new relationship. He was responsible for all the supplies of the colony: trading for them, overseeing them, arranging for rationing if necessary. He was the colony's accountant (though at times Isaac Allerton took on these duties); the secretary of state, who made

Women tending one of the many garden plots so essential to the colonists.
Even Bradford did his share of fieldwork. *(reenactment photo)*

treaties and received visitors; the head of the military in charge of defense. He assigned tasks in the community, looked to the inventories, dealt with discharging the Merchant Adventurers' debt, oversaw the shipping in the bay, sent out trading expeditions, and kept an account of the colony's needs. He was judge and jury, the one who interpreted the law and saw that it was carried out. In addition, he took his turn in the fields and in the forests, hoeing and sawing with all the other colonists.

But what is most remarkable about this man who played all of these roles is that he was beloved of the colonists. He never played the dictator or tyrant, and he never took a position higher than the others. He was the colony's servant, and his leadership was a leadership of service.

Soon after Bradford was elected governor again, Edward Winslow returned in Weston's ship, aptly named the *Charity*. He brought with him something the Pilgrims had not seen since leaving Europe: three heifers and a bull, "the first begining of any catle of that kind in the land," wrote Bradford. With the arrival of the cattle, the Pilgrims gave up forever the idea of living off the sea as fishermen, "a thing fatall to this plantation," Bradford wrote. Winslow had brought over supplies as well, these gathered together by Robert Cushman. Believing that they would still be fishermen, Cushman had sent nets and hooks; these would not be used as often as he intended. He also sent over items to trade with the Indians, as well as a ship carpenter, a salt maker, and other colonists recruited by the Merchant Adventurers.

The ship carpenter began to construct a series of small vessels: two ketches with two masts, an open and flat-bottomed boat called a lighter, and six or seven larger rigged boats (shallops). Cushman advised that the carpenter be given "absolute command over his servants & such as are put to him." He went to work quickly and soon began to produce the boats that would later be so important, not to fishing, but to trading. Unfortunately, he died that summer.

The salt maker was a failure. The Pilgrims had hoped that he would be able to produce enough salt that the colony could send salted fish back to the English market. But even if they had caught fish, the salt maker never fully understood the "misterie" of his craft. Eventually he burned down the building that had been erected for him. Bradford, who hated boasters and men who spoke well but effected little, called him "an ignorante, foolish, self-willd fellow" but allowed him to continue his work for two reasons: because it was not interfering with the tasks of the colony, and because some among the Strangers might have written back to the Merchant Adventurers to claim that Bradford would not allow the salt maker to finish what he had begun.

And here is a hint, for the first time, that Bradford sensed that some among the Plymouth colonists still saw themselves as very much apart from the Leyden folk. In fact, this separation became much more obvious with the presence of John Lyford, yet another minister from the Church of England whom the Merchant Adventurers had sent over instead of John Robinson. The Adventurers, it seemed, feared the growing dominance of the Leyden congregation, and were more and more reluctant to send any of them over. "Our hopes of coming unto you be small and weaker than ever," wrote John Robinson in a letter that Winslow carried. "The Adventurers, it seems, have neither money nor any great mind of us, for the most parte." They refused to transport any more of the Leyden group, and were more interested, Robinson wrote, in bringing over Puritan preachers. Hence the presence of John Lyford.

Bradford was incensed; he had waited so long for his pastor to come over. But yet again, he showed good grace to the presence of Lyford, even though he represented a threat to the Separatist cause. Still, his coming apparently pleased the Strangers among the colonists, and his first impression upon the Saints was not a bad one, though he seemed overly humble: "When this man first came a shore, he saluted them with that reverence and humilitie as is seldom to be seen, and indeed made them ashamed, he so bowed and cringed unto them, and would have kissed their hands if they would have suffered him." As a clergyman, he was given the best house in town, as well as the largest food allowance. A servant was assigned to him, and though he was a newcomer, he was allowed to sit at the council along with William Brewster to decide matters of government.

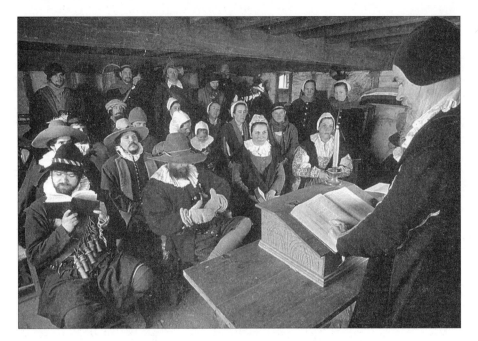

Colonists gathered for a church service *(reenactment photo)*

For the rest of his governorship, which was to last well more than thirty years, Bradford would try his utmost to maintain the vision that had begun Plymouth Colony and had sustained it through its early, terrible winter. In these early days, he did not realize the kinds of challenges that would come after he had made peace with the Indians, fought off starvation, and dispatched with rival traders.

But the first of these new challenges to Plymouth's vision was Lyford himself. Within a week, he asked to be admitted to the Separatist church, which both Bradford and Brewster found remarkable; after all, here was an Anglican clergyman casting aside what he himself called "many corruptions which had been a burthen to his conscience" and his "former disorderly walking." He was welcomed, and soon he was sharing the pulpit with Brewster, taking the place, as it were, of John Robinson.

But very soon, Bradford began to notice small groups forming and whispering; private meetings were held, and a group of those who had always been complainers gathered around Lyford, who listened to and encouraged their complaints, "were they never so vile nor profane." When the Hiltons, a family among the Strangers, had a child, they went to Lyford for the baptism, since they were Anglicans and not part of the Plymouth church, and since Brewster, not being an ordained minister, could not baptize the baby. Lyford took charge and baptized the child.

It was also noted that Lyford was busy about his writing, and when one afternoon the *Charity* weighed anchor and headed out into the bay, bound for England with supplies, Bradford put out in the shallop and stopped the ship out of sight of Plymouth. Aboard, he discovered letters Lyford had written to the Merchant Adventurers, "full of slanders & false accusations, tending not only to their prejudice, but to their ruine & utter subversion." Bradford copied all the letters and kept several of the originals. Upon his return, Bradford said nothing.

Things finally came to a head when John Oldham, one of Lyford's closest associates, refused to take his turn to stand guard. In the ensuing quarrel with Miles Standish, Oldham drew his knife and finally had to be subdued and imprisoned in the fort, for, as Bradford wrote, he "ramped more like a furious beast than a man, and cald them all traitours, and rebells, and other such foule language." Lyford decided that he would make his move; "without ever speaking one word either to the Governor, Church, or Elder," he "set up a publick meeting aparte, on the Lord's day." Had Lyford been trying to offend, he could hardly have done so more effectively.

Bradford had had enough. Both Lyford and Oldham were called to trial for "plotting against them and disturbing their peace, both in respecte of their civill & church state, which was most injurious, for both they and all the world knew they came hither to injoye the libertie of conscience and the free use of God's ordinances." At first both were insolent, saying that Bradford had no proof of his charges. Then Bradford drew out the letters and, in the stunned silence that followed, began to read the slanders that Lyford had written. The silence must have been especially profound when Lyford advised the Merchant Adventurers to send over as many Strangers as possible so that they might overwhelm the Separatists by mere numbers. It was especially important, Lyford wrote, that "the Leyden company (Mr. Robinson & the rest) must be kepte back, or els all will be spoyled."

In the silence that followed, Lyford burst into tears. He claimed that he had been deceived, that he had only written what others had told him. He now saw that he was terribly wrong, and that he was nothing but "unsavorie salt." Bradford agreed; he was unsavory salt, and like all such salt he must be cast aside.

Both Lyford and Oldham were banished to other colonies along the eastern coast, Oldham immediately, Lyford after six months. Anything that clouded the purity of Plymouth's vision, Bradford felt, had to be wiped out. There seems to have been no resistance on the part of the Strangers at Plymouth to his judgment. Even they saw the necessity of holding the colony to the dream that had maintained it so far; their frequent election of Bradford to the governorship showed this as well.

But with Lyford disposed of, Bradford as governor realized that the Merchant Adventurers would never stop meddling in Plymouth's affairs, since they saw it as their own colony. Something would have to be done to break the tie. Bradford sent Miles Standish over in 1625 to speak with Ferdinando Gorges, to see if there might not be some way to free Plymouth from the Adventurers, who were still complaining that the Pilgrims "suffer all the general goods and affairs to go at sixes and sevens and spend your time in idleness."

Gorges was no help, so Standish approached the Adventurers themselves. But there had been a terrible outburst of plague in London that summer, and they were doing almost no business. They were in no mood to grant much to the Pilgrims anyway, for, though Standish had brought the *Little James* with him, loaded with some cod and many beaver pelts — enough to pay off more than a quarter of the entire debt — that ship had been stolen in the English Channel by Barbary pirates, another complete loss.

Nevertheless, Standish returned to Plymouth in the spring of 1626, having begun negotiations to end all ties with the Merchant Adventurers. The Pilgrims planned to buy out their shares in the colony and to repay them over nine years. Later, Isaac Allerton traveled to London to complete the negotiations, and his return must have been marked by rejoicing from Bradford, for it marked the end of the Adventurers' meddling.

But when Standish returned, he also brought news that deeply affected the colony. First, their old enemy King James was dead, and Charles I was on the English throne. Second, Robert Cushman, who had made so many plans for the Pilgrims, had died in London of the plague. And finally, and most devastating, John Robinson had died in Leyden. Though he was such a part of the Pilgrim vision, he had never come to the New World, nor seen the colony that was so much a part of his vision. Bradford had lost two close friends, and his household mourned. The days were especially dark because Bradford had invited Cushman's son Thomas to live in his household, and now Thomas mourned his father.

But as he had once before, Bradford had to put his mourning

aside. The colonists now had an even larger debt to pay off to the Merchant Adventurers, since they had bought out their controlling shares. Bradford sent Edward Winslow north to Maine, where he opened trade with the Abnaki Indians along the Kennebec River. He sent Winslow up to Cape Ann, where the Pilgrims established another trading post near the Massachusett Indians. And the Pilgrims traveled below Cape Cod, where they set up trade with the Wampanoags and Narragansetts at Aptucxet. As they pushed farther and farther south, they encountered the settlements of the Dutch, who apparently did not feel threatened by the Pilgrims. Peter Minuit, the governor of New Netherlands, wrote to Bradford with advice and sent wampum to help with trade, which, Bradford wrote, "turned most of their advantage."

But in the middle of all this work, as the colony began to prosper, Bradford missed his son John, who was still back in the Netherlands. Pastor Robinson had been his father, and now he had died. Bradford himself had never known what it was like to have a father, and perhaps he had not known what he was keeping from his son. But he knew now. Already he had established a very close relationship with Thomas Cushman, much like what William Brewster had with him when he was a teenager. (In fact, Thomas would follow William Brewster as the ruling elder, and he would remain in Plymouth at that post for over forty years, until 1691.) And there were others in his household who called his fatherly duties to mind.

By the time Bradford sent for John in 1627, he had a new mother to meet, as well as a new half brother and half sister. But Bradford never had the time to devote to John that the boy needed. Soon after his arrival, Alice sent for her two children, Constant and Thomas, both around John's age of nine or ten. In addition, at least one of George Morton's five children was living with the Bradford household, George having died three years earlier; Nathaniel Morton was also just about John's age. In fact, by 1628, there were nine children from five different interconnected families living with Bradford and Alice. It was difficult for John, coming from Leyden and entering a close household as a stranger, to find his way into the routines and relationships.

The sight of John must have brought to Bradford's mind the long-gone Dorothy and other, deeper feelings: the sense of being a young boy who has lost something he can never recover, the sense of being deserted, of being a stranger in one's own home. Bradford had known the pain of these feelings, but it seems that he was able to do little to help his own son deal with them. Though Bradford's other children became important in the colony in later years, John never did. He would eventually marry a woman named Martha Bourne and leave Plymouth for Duxbury, then Marshfield, and finally Norwich, Connecticut, and never have any children of his own. It was a sadness that must have cut deeply into Bradford.

But if all was not altogether well in his own household, Bradford could look upon his work in Plymouth and smile. In 1627, Plymouth had grown to about 180 people, with thirty-two houses, a fort, a storehouse, a wharf, and a graveyard. Trading up and down the coast was brisk, and supplies were coming in now from Britain.

The town itself was well established. The "street" ran up from the bay to the fort; the "road" ran at right angles along the coast. At the crossroads stood Bradford's house, diagonally across from William Brewster's. Isaac de Rasieres, a visitor from the Dutch colony down south by "the Manhatas," was most impressed by Plymouth:

> Their houses are constructed of hewn planks [or clapboards], with gardens also enclosed behind and at the sides with hewn planks, so that their houses and court-yeards are arranged in very good order, with a stockade against a sudden attack, and at the

In good times and bad, the chores of daily life were endless. *(reenactment photo)*

end of the streets there are three wooden gates. In the center, on the cross street, stands the Governor's house, before which is a square enclosure, upon which four patereros [cannons] are mounted, so as to flank along the streets. . . . Their farms are not as good as ours because they are more stony and consequently not so suitable for the plough. . . . They have better means of living than ourselves because they have the fish so abundant before their doors.

If de Rasieres had known about the Pilgrims' lack of success with fishing, he might not have said this. His comment about the poor farming, however, was to be prophetic.

Life was easier now, but not easy. The small houses stood closely together, and the kitchen gardens behind them required con-

Spreading out laundry to dry on the grass *(reenactment photo)*

stant watering by hand. Though the colonists had taken with them some ornate pieces of wooden furniture, everything else in the homes was plain and humble, so that a beautifully carved chair might stand beside a worn straw mattress. Furthermore, after all this time, no one's training in anything other than farming was used, with the exception perhaps of William Brewster. Chores were constant; ease was nonexistent.

And more trials lay ahead.

Bradford still hoped more of the Leyden congregation would join them eventually, despite the death of John Robinson. In 1630, the last of the Leyden congregation to come to Plymouth arrived aboard the *Handmaid* — sixty of the Saints. But Bradford, thinking as a governor more than a Saint, was not particularly happy to see these pilgrims, not because they represented more mouths to feed, but because they were "without any of note and better discretion and government amongst them." He never bothered to record their names or how they were dispersed among the thirty-two houses. From his perspective, they did the colony little good. Still, he wrote, "they were such as feared God."

He would need more useful people, because the challenges he faced as governor were still not ended. From the south and from the north, rival colonies began to pressure Plymouth. Bradford could not ignore these rivals; the debt was even greater now, and so was the need to expand the trade in beaver pelts. Rival colonies meant fewer pelts and higher trading prices — neither of which Plymouth could afford.

Bradford felt he could act aggressively against these rivals, especially against the colony established somewhat north of them by Captain Wollaston and Thomas Morton, who brought with them a crew of indentured servants — those who paid for their passage by agreeing to work for the colony for a number of years. They settled — insolently and illegally, the Pilgrims felt — on land that the Pilgrims themselves claimed, naming it Mount Wollaston after the captain. But there was never any strong guiding hand like that of Bradford in Mount Wollaston, and by the spring of 1628 Wollaston and Morton had quarreled, Morton had taken over as the head of the trading post, Wollaston had left, and the site had been renamed Merry-Mount.

But they were not laughing for very long. When the Pilgrims learned about the quarrel, they were disturbed indeed, not because they favored Wollaston, but because of the results of Morton's conspiring. He had told the indentured servants that they could rid themselves of Wollaston's rule and would then "be free from service, and we will converse, trad, plante, and live together as equalls." This they readily accepted, and the Pilgrims themselves would have understood the desire to live as equals, though they would not have approved throwing over an honest debt. But what followed alarmed them:

> After this they fell to great licenciousnes, and led a dissolute life, powering out them selves into all profanenes. And Morton became lord of misrule, and maintained (as it were) a schoole of Ath[e]isme. And after they gott some good into their hands, and gott much by trading with the Indeans, they spent it as vainly, in quaffing and drinking both wine and strong waters in great exsess. . . . They also set up a May-pole, drinking and dancing aboute it many days togeather, inviting the Indean women, for their consorts, dancing and frisking togither.

The notion of this kind of colony so close to Plymouth was appalling to Bradford. It went against the vision that had guided Plymouth, and he certainly feared its influence upon his own people — much as Robinson and Brewster had feared the effects of the looser Netherlandish culture on their young ones.

But there were other reasons to see Morton's colony as a threat. "Now to maintaine this riotous prodigallitie and profuse excess, Morton, thinking him selfe lawless, and hearing what gaine the French and fisher-men made by trading of peeces [guns], powder, and shotte to the Indeans, he, as the head of this consortship, began the practise of the same in these parts; and first he taught them how to use them, to charge, and discharg, and what proportion of powder to give the peece, according to the size or bignes of the same." Morton began to employ the Indians to shoot for him, and they were apparently much taken by guns, "accounting their bowes and arrowes but baubles in comparison of them."

Bradford confronting the revelers at Merry-Mount

There were two dangers here. First, the Indians were now much better armed and, consequently, much more of a threat to Plymouth. Second, the Indians, eager to acquire more guns, were bringing their pelts to Merry-Mount to trade — and enjoying the strong waters that accompanied the trading.

When Bradford heard that Morton had started to send to England for more guns, he knew that the colony had to be stopped. Bradford gathered his council, and with them sent two letters to Morton, asking, and then demanding, that this trade in guns be stopped, "for the countrie could not beare the injure he did; it was against their comone saftie." Morton at first denied the trade, and then declared he would do what he would, and "if any came to molest him, let them looke to them selves, for he would prepare for them."

These were the same words that Bradford himself had used to bluff his way past a possible attack by Canonicus and the Narragansetts. But Bradford was not Canonicus; he sent Miles Standish to Merry-Mount with a picked group of men. There they found Morton and his crew barricaded within the trading post. Standish hollered that they should yield, but scornful replies came back. Finally, Morton decided to attack, and his crew ran from the house but were too drunk to shoot their weapons. Standish himself stepped up to Morton and jerked his gun away. The only injury went to one of Morton's men who, in his drunkenness, "rane his owne nose upon the pointe of a sword that one held before him as he entred the house; but he lost but a litle of his hott blood."

Standish brought Morton back to Plymouth and kept him there until a ship sailed back to England. He was bundled aboard, along with letters about his activities, and sailed out of Plymouth harbor. His colony dispersed, yet another threat gone from Plymouth — though the guns he had traded remained and, Bradford wrote, would continue to do much damage. But in the end, Morton's colony was only a small threat. As Bradford pondered on how he might keep the vision of Plymouth alive — and by this he meant the physical town, both in terms of its economic activity and its spiritual life — he would have to face even greater challenges from more skilled rivals.

NINE

"I Shall Doe What I Can"

With Morton gone, the beaver trade began to flourish; by the 1630s, Bradford might have been able to say it was thriving. After terrible struggle, the colony was finally well established. But there were disturbing hints that the colony would never grow much beyond what it already was; the Leyden congregation was simply too poor to continue to send over ships with new colonists. The Plymouth population had reached three hundred, but it would not grow larger, and would in fact begin to decline. Early in the 1630s Bradford must have begun to understand that the colony was in danger of being swallowed up by other, better-financed, more aggressive colonies. Much of the remaining years of his governorship entailed struggles to keep Plymouth distinct and independent.

This would not be easy. Just to the north, the Puritans — those who had decided to stay within the Church of England and reform it from the inside — had begun to settle in Massachusetts Bay. The

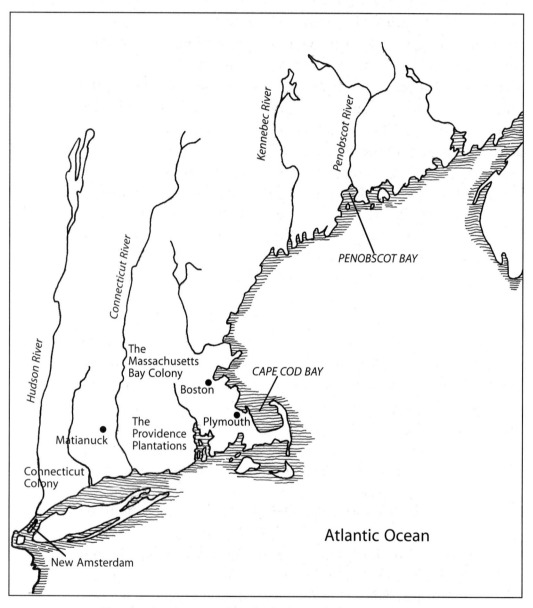

Map showing the encroachment of other settlements on Plymouth

first ship, the *Abigail*, had arrived on the coast in 1628, carrying the minister John Endecott, who, with six other "religious" persons, had purchased a patent for the Massachusetts Bay area from Ferdinando Gorges's Council for New England. Well financed, the Puritans began to come over in droves; in 1630 alone, thirteen ships brought over one thousand colonists, more than triple the number of little Plymouth to the south.

At first, relations between the two colonies were quite good. Upon first arriving, Endecott and his colonists were devastated by disease and, like the Pilgrims, lost half of their group. They desperately appealed to Plymouth for help, and Bradford sent Samuel Fuller, their "physition & chirurgeon [surgeon]." Fuller mended their bodies, but in addition he spoke of the Separatist ways of Plymouth, until Endecott, recognizing how far away they were from England now, was convinced. Here was a people, he found, who worshiped God truly, and who were completely unlike the stories that were still told about them back in England. Endecott wrote to Bradford, thanking him for Fuller and, especially, for a new vision of his religious life.

> God's people are all marked with one and the same marke, and sealed with one and the same seale, and have for the mayne one & the same hart, guided by one & the same spirite of truth; and where this is, there can be no discorde; nay, here must needs be sweete harmonie. I acknowledge myself much bound to you for your kind love and care in sending Mr. Fuller among us, and rejoyce much that I am by him satisfied touching your judgements of the outward forme of God's worshipe. It is, as farr as I can yet gather, no other than is warrented by the evidence of truth . . . being farr from the commone reporte that hath been spread of you touching that perticuler.

165

Bradford and other Pilgrims rejoiced.

Perhaps the Plymouth colonists sensed that the Puritans would eventually dominate them by their sheer numbers. And perhaps they sensed that the Massachusetts Bay Colony would swallow them, until Plymouth was no longer independent. But this would not happen for sixty years, and even when it did, the Pilgrim vision of the religious life would be the one to survive.

Within a year the Puritans were embracing the same form of services as the Pilgrims, and, most dramatic of all, were electing their own ministers — something that would never be allowed in the Church of England. They had begun the movement that would lead to the congregationalism — the notion that each church should govern itself — that would dominate New England in the next century.

But within a very short time, relations between the colonies began to sour — not over religious matters, in which the two colonies would always remain close, but over economic matters. The Puritans were always better financed, with better tools, supplies, and goods to trade. They began to cast their eyes over the fur trade around them, and saw that it could become quite profitable. In addition, their size allowed them to begin to lord themselves over Plymouth.

In 1634, a John Hocking encroached upon a Pilgrim trading post on the Kennebec River in Maine. In the angry exchanges that followed, Hocking shot one of the Pilgrim men who was sent by John Alden to cut the cables of Hocking's ship, forcing it away. Hocking himself was then shot and killed. When Alden later put in at Boston on his way back to Plymouth, he was arrested by the Puritan governor, John Winthrop.

Plymouth angrily sent Miles Standish to bring him back, but the Puritans detained Standish as well, as one who could testify about the Pilgrims' patent for the Kennebec. Plymouth was furious; Winthrop countered that the incident "has brought us all and the gospel under the common reproach of cutting one another's throats for Beaver." Someone needed to show that things were under control, lest the king send over a royal governor, and neither side wanted that. Alden was eventually acquitted and returned with Standish to Plymouth, and though peace was again established, Bradford did not forget that the Massachusetts Bay Colony had assumed the right to make judgments over Plymouth.

Soon afterward the Pilgrims suffered another attack on one of their outposts, this by the French on the trading post at Penobscot, also in Maine. Bradford went to the Puritan colony for help, but none was offered. Instead, some of the Puritan merchants immediately went north and began to trade with the French, and Bradford was astonished and dismayed at what he saw as a betrayal. By trading with the French, Bradford wrote, "it is no marvell that they still grow, & incroach more & more upon the English, and fill the Indeans with gunes & munition, to the great deanger of the English." The danger, of course, was much greater to the smaller Plymouth colony than to Massachusetts Bay. The Pilgrims reluctantly abandoned the Penobscot trading post, an enormous financial loss. But even more, they saw that Massachusetts Bay was no real ally, and instead a very large and powerful rival.

This was soon confirmed. The Pilgrims had established a trading post at Matianuck, on the Connecticut River; it was managed by Jonathan Brewster, William's son. But in 1634, a settlement came out from the Puritans and planted itself firmly by the Pilgrims' post. Bradford warned them that they were trespassing and told Jonathan Brewster that he should be kind but firm. Brewster promised that "I

167

Of plimoth plantation

And first of y occasion, and Indusments ther unto; the which that y may truly unfould, y must begine at y very roote & rise of y same. the which y shall endeuor to manefest in a plaine stile; with singuler regard unto y simple trueth in all things, at least as near as my slender Judgmente can attaine the same.

1. Chapter

It is well knowne unto y godly, and judicious, how euer since y first breaking out of y lighte of y gospell, in our Honourable nation of England (which was y first of nations, whom y Lord adorned ther with, after y grose darknes of popery which had couered, & ouerspred y Christian worled) what warrs, & oppositions euer since satan hath raised, maintained, and continued against the saincts, from time, to time in one sorte, or other. Some times by bloody death & cruell torments, other whiles ymprisonments, banishments, & other hard usages. As being loath his kingdom should goe downe, the trueth preuaile; and y Churches of god reuerte to thai anciente puritie; and recouer, their primatiue order, libertie & bewtie. But when he could not preuaile by these means, against the maine trueths of y gospell, but that they began to take rooting in many places; being watered with y blood of y martires, and blesed from heauen with a gracious encrease. He then begune to take him to his anciente strategemes, used of old against the first Christians. That when by y bloody, & barbarous persecutions of y Heathen Emperours, he could not stoppe, & subuerte the course of y gospell; but that it spedily ouerspred, with a wounderfull celeritie, the then best known parts of y world. He then begane to sow errours, heresies, and wounderfull disentions amongst y proffessours them selues (working upon their pride, & ambition, with other corrupte pasions, yncidente to all mortall men; yea to y saints them selues in some measure) By which wofull effects followed; as not only bitter contentions, & hartburnings, schismes, with other horrible confusions. But satan tooke occasion, & aduantage therby to foyst in a number of vile ceremoneys, with many unprofitable cannons, & decrees which haue since been as snares, to many poore, & peacable souls, euen to this day. So as in y anciente times, the persecuti-

A page from *Of Plymouth Plantation*, in which Bradford faithfully recorded both the hardships and the blessings of the colony

shall doe what I can to withstand them," but it was to no avail, for, Brewster wrote back to Bradford, "they are comming dayly." Bradford wrote to Boston: "We tould you before and (upon this occasion) must tell you still, that our mind is otherwise, and that you cast rather a partiall, if not a covetous eye, upon that which is your neighbour's and not yours. . . . Looke that ye abuse not God's providence in such allegations."

God's providence, answered the Puritans, had led them to this place, "the Lord's waste . . . void of inhabitants." But Bradford insisted that the Puritans had been told that Plymouth intended to colonize those "waste" lands, and that they were in fact stealing them. The Puritans could settle there, he claimed justly, only because they were better supplied than the Pilgrims, but that gave them no justification. But Winthrop would not move.

Bradford was in a quandary; the only way to retain the lands would be to remove the Puritans with force, much as they had done with Thomas Morton. But John Winthrop was no Thomas Morton, and Bradford had no desire to live in angry contention. "To make any forcible resistance was farr from their thoughts . . . and to live in continuall contention with their freinds and brethren would be uncomfortable, and too heavie a burden to bear. Therfore for peace sake . . . they thought it better to let them have it upon as good termes as they could gett; and so they fell to treaty." The Pilgrims kept the post and a small parcel of land, and received some money for the land they surrendered to the Puritans. But here was yet another source of funding gone. "Thus was the controversie ended, but the unkindnes not so soone forgotten," Bradford concludes. The hurt was deep indeed, for it was unlike Bradford to hold the grudge for long.

If Bradford remembered the unkindness, he did not show it to the Puritans. In 1636, two ships heading out from Boston with supplies for the intruding settlement were hit by a storm and thrown upon the Plymouth coastline. "The boats men were lost, and the goods were driven all alonge the shore, and strowed up and downe at highwater marke." Bradford had all of the goods gathered up and an inventory made. He had them washed and dried and returned to the Puritans. His was a gracious response, but he saw in the ship-wrecks the hand of God. "Such crosses they mette with in their beginings; which some imputed as a correction from God for their intrution (to the wrong of others) into that place. But I dare not be bould with Gods judgements in this kind." But even if he would not be bold enough to claim that God had punished the Puritans, clearly he felt the justice of their difficulties.

But things were still not at an end with the colony the Puritans had established in Connecticut. In 1637, the Pequot Indians attacked it and "slew sundry of them, (as they were at work in the feilds,) both men and women, to the great terrour of the rest; and went away in great prid and triumph, with many high threats." John Winthrop, up in Boston, assumed that Plymouth would come to their aid, and Bradford began to make preparations — though with some reluc-tance. Perhaps he agreed because he heard that the Pequots were trying to turn the Narragansetts against all the English, whom they feared would "overspred their countrie."

So troops from Plymouth, Connecticut, and Massachusetts Bay traveled to the trading post, and together with their Narragansett al-lies marched through the night to the encampment of the Pequots. Surrounding it, they set on fire the windward side of the encamp-ment, the wind carrying the flames in a rushing blaze. Most were killed by the flames and shots fired into the camp, and some were killed by Pilgrim swords, so that in the end four hundred died, and the threat against the Puritan outpost was destroyed.

Bradford's Bible, one of his greatest treasures

Bradford's exultation in this victory seems to go against his character. His vivid description of the scene is horrific, yet gloating: "It was a fearfull sight to see them thus frying in the fyer, and the streams of blood quenching the same, and horrible was the stinck and sente ther of." There is an Old Testament delight in the destruction of enemies, and Bradford's pleasure here is not so much in the physical slaughter as in the evidence of God's continued care over the Pilgrims: "They gave the prays therof to God, who wrought so wonderfuly for them, thus to inclose their enimise in their hands, and give them so speedy a victory over so proud and insulting an enimie."

Little would change as the years went by. Bradford would continue to hold on to his dream of Plymouth's independence, while the Puritans would whittle away at it, taking over more and more territory. In 1639 and 1640, the Puritan town of Hingham claimed land that was clearly within the boundary of Plymouth Colony; in fact, the line drawn on one map claimed some of Plymouth village itself for Hingham. Hingham argued that its patent was for all land three miles south of the Charles River, and it called all rivers and tributaries that flowed into the Charles part of the river itself. It took two years for the two colonies to settle the dispute, again with loss of land for Plymouth.

Even as the Pilgrims were sorting out their relationships with the Puritans, there was also pressure in Connecticut from the Dutch, who had always been friendly. In 1633, when the Pilgrims were trying to settle along the Connecticut River, the Dutch saw them as intruding farther south than they had a right. In fact, by penetrating farther into the river than the Dutch had, it was likely, thought the Dutch, that the Pilgrims would hurt the Dutch trade. So when the Pilgrims came to establish their trading post, the Dutch demanded their withdrawal and threatened to attack. The Pilgrims went on and built a small fort where they intended to settle. Finally the Dutch "sent a band of about 70. men, in warrlike maner, with collours displayed, to assaulte them; but seeing them strengthened, and that it would cost blood, they came to parley, and returned in peace." Bradford does not reveal the terms of that parley that led to peace, but in any event, the Dutch felt as wounded by the Pilgrims as the Pilgrims had by the Puritans. The Dutch, too, would remember the unkindness.

Up north, the Pilgrims were even harder pressed by the French in their trading posts in Maine. In 1631, the French robbed the Pilgrims' trading post at Penobscot. Arriving while the master of the post was gone, they pretended to be newly come from the sea in a leaky vessel. When they all had landed, they came into the post and, as they seemed to be interested in purchasing muskets, suddenly turned a gun on the servants who had been left in charge. They carried away three hundred pounds of beaver pelts, coats, rugs, blankets, biscuits, and other trading goods. They left, leaving only mockery behind them.

It was yet another loss that the Pilgrims could ill afford. But the loss four years later was even more devastating. A Monsieur de Aulnay, who was asked by the French government to drive out intruders into Maine, stopped a shallop carrying the agents of the trading post and compelled them to pilot him into the bay. There he took over the house and forced the agents to sell him all their goods at a price that he set, telling them he would pay at a convenient time if they would come for the money; the agents knew he had no intention of ever paying. Aulnay told them the post itself and all its fortifications were forfeit to the French, "saing that they which build on another mans ground doe forfite the same." So he turned them out, allowing them the shallop and a few provisions to sail back to Plymouth.

Outraged, Bradford asked the Puritans for help in getting the station back; the Puritans agreed only if the Pilgrims would pay for the entire expedition, and Bradford, probably with a sigh, agreed. They sent a boat up to the Penobscot, with Miles Standish in charge of the Plymouth men, but when they approached, the ship's captain fired off most of his powder while he was still far away, doing no damage. When they neared the shore, he had no powder to protect Standish during the landing. The mission having failed, the Pilgrims again asked for the Puritans' aid, but in Bradford's kind words, "this came to nothing."

Assailed from the north by the Puritans and the French, assailed from the south by the Dutch, always with an eye to the west against the Pequots and any other warring tribe, the Pilgrims must have felt that, even though they had conquered hunger, they could never be secure in this colony. Bradford knew that he would always have to be vigilant against the greater, greedier colonies all around him.

But Bradford did not suspect, perhaps, that Plymouth would be assailed from within as well — and this because of success. In the early 1630s, Plymouth families began to grow rich, not only because they had finally discovered the secrets of farming in New England, but because their trade was flourishing. Corn and cattle and other supplies became more and more valuable as other settlers came to the New World, particularly in the early days of Boston, where so many people were coming so quickly. As their trade became more and more profitable, so their farms grew larger and larger. This meant that if the Plymouth folk were to tend to their flocks and cattle, they would have to leave the town itself and live out on their estates, in newly built houses. In addition, if they were to keep larger herds, they would need more land for grazing — and this, too, meant leaving the town of Plymouth. Bradford felt the colonists were losing some of the religious vision that had brought them to the New World and had substituted for it a drive for wealth: "And no man now thought he could live, except he had catle and a great deale of ground to keep them; all striving to increase their flocks." Very soon, the colonists were scattered all over the Plymouth Bay region, "and the towne, in which they lived compactly till now, was left very thinn, and in a short time allmost desolate."

An even harder blow was the division of the Plymouth church. As families moved away from Plymouth, it became harder for them to travel back into town for the Sunday services. In 1632 a group living on the other side of Plymouth Bay asked to be dismissed from the Plymouth church so that they might meet together in what would be called "Duxberie." Bradford very reluc-

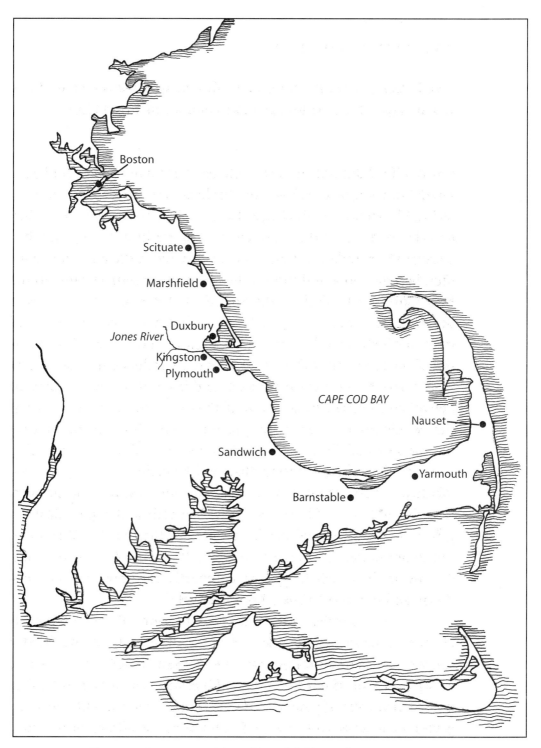

The price of success: wealthy residents left Plymouth to start new towns

tantly agreed, referring to it as a "sadd matter." He felt that this would allow others to break away more easily, and in this he was right. It meant the loss of one of the central goals of their journey to New England: united and unhindered worship. "And this, I fear, will be the ruine of New-England, at least of the churches of God ther, and will provock the Lords displeasure against them." Where Bradford had not been bold enough to proclaim God's judgment against the Puritans for their theft of the Connecticut trading post, he was indeed bold enough to suggest God's will at the loss of something much dearer and more important to him.

The decade of the 1630s ended ominously with a "great and fearfull earthquake." "It came with rumbling noyse, or low murmure, like unto remoate thunder; it came from the norward, and pased southward. As the noyse aproched nerer, the earth begane to shake, and came at length with that violence as caused platters, dishes, and such like things as stoode upon shelves, to clatter and fall downe; yea, persons were afraid of the houses themselves." An after-shock came through half an hour later, and Bradford observed that for several years afterward the summers were cooler than normal, and the corn did not mature as well. But, as in all things, Bradford saw the hand of God in the earthquake. "So powerfull is the mighty hand of the Lord, as to make both the earth and sea to shake, and the mountaines to tremble before him, when he pleases; and who can stay his hand?" Perhaps, as Bradford wrote these words, he was thinking that nothing would destroy God's work in Plymouth itself, for who could stay God's hand there?

But, it seemed, Plymouth was not to be the kind of town Bradford hoped for; the dispersal of families continued. Duxbury was founded by families leaving Plymouth, then Marshfield, Scituate, Sandwich, Barnstable, and Yarmouth, moving farther and farther up the arm of the cape. Finally, in the middle of the 1640s, came the

Building in Duxbury: John Alden's house (above) and the Standish home (below)

proposal that Bradford must have been dreading: Plymouth, it was said, was now too barren to support a growing population; the town itself should be abandoned and the families settled in a new, more fertile place.

Bradford was aghast, though his position was a difficult one: though the residence of the governor was to always be in Plymouth town, Bradford himself had built a new house in Kingston to be closer to the fields that he owned and, for a time, worked with tenant farmers. He himself was contributing to the dispersal.

But Bradford argued against the proposal. Still, the challenge was a telling one: Boston was only half the age of Plymouth, yet it supported a population now five times that of Plymouth. Bradford's answer, and the answer of slightly fewer than half of the other colonists, was one of tradition only: This was the place they had worked so hard to build, where the next generation had been born. Indeed, he argued, "men might hear live, if they would be contente with their condition; and that it was not for wante or necessitie so much that they removed, as for the enriching of them selves." This was not a fair accusation, and Bradford himself must have felt the hypocrisy of it, but he was desperately searching for a way to preserve the town.

Thomas Prence, who had been chosen as governor in 1634 and 1638 when Bradford had asked for some relief, led those who wished to remove, and a site was chosen not far from Nauset. Plymouth Colony agreed to yield the land, and further rights were purchased from the Indians. It seemed that Plymouth would come to an end.

But at the last moment, a reprieve. After a careful survey, it became clear that the new site would only support twenty-five families at the most. It would not be capable of any increase, "as (at least in a shorte time) they should be worse ther then they are now hear." The plan was formally abandoned, but some of those who had started refused to be put off, and so the new town was founded anyway, led

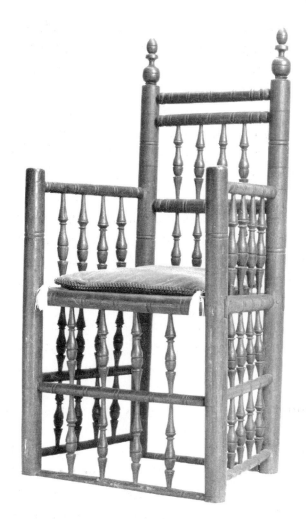

Bradford's chair, which
he may have used in
his "studdie"

by Thomas Prence and six other families. It would eventually become the town of Eastham.

It was yet another blow struck at the town of Plymouth. "And thus was this poore church left, like an anciente mother, grown olde, and forsaken of her children, (though not in their affections,) yet in regarde of their bodily presence and personall helpfulness. Her anciente members being most of them worne away by death; and these of later time being like children translated into other families, and she like a widow left only to trust in God. Thus she that had made many rich became her selfe poore." Poor indeed. By the middle of the 1640s Plymouth Colony had 3,000 residents; only 150 of these lived in Plymouth town. The town had about the same number of people it had in 1623.

As Bradford wrote about the "anciente mother," Plymouth, he might also have been thinking about his own family. The house that he and Alice shared now accommodated Bradford's first son, John; Bradford and Alice's four children; Bradford's two stepchildren; Alice's nephew Nathaniel Morton; and four orphan boys — twelve children all told, children Bradford himself taught as schoolmaster. But they were now marrying and leaving the Bradford household.

Nathaniel Morton, who had been Bradford's secretary, was one of the first to leave, becoming clerk of the colony for forty years. In the late 1630s Alice's sons were married, and both would go on to become important men in Duxbury and Plymouth, Thomas finally as assistant governor. In 1640 Bradford's son John married and moved to Duxbury. Among the orphans Bradford had taken in, Joseph Rogers married and moved to Eastham, William Lathan returned to England, and Sam Cuthbertson was apprenticed to a tailor and moved in with that family. Since the Bradfords had increased the size of their home to accommodate all the children — adding a new bedroom for Bradford and Alice, as well as a "great rome" or "studdie" — the house now must have seemed too large with only five or six people left.

As if this were not enough, Bradford had a growing conviction that Plymouth, as a town founded on a way of worship that included all of life, was losing its vision, even its faith. In 1642 he wrote plaintively, "Marvilous it may be to see and consider how some kind of wickednes did grow and breake forth here, in a land wher the same was so much witnesed against, and so narrowly looked unto, and severly punished when it was knowne; as in no place more, or so much, that I have known or heard of; insomuch as they have been somewhat censured, even by moderate and good men. . . . And yet all this could not suppress the breaking out of sundrie notorious sins."

Bradford looked around for an answer to this loosening of the vision, and first turned to the most obvious place: humanity's corruptible nature. But he came back as well to the old problem of the Saints and Strangers. Though the Saints had come over to found a city on a hill, they had brought with them others who came for other reasons, those who had come for profit. "And by this means the cuntrie became pestered with many unworthy persons, who, being come over, crept into one place or other." Bradford concluded that this was the affliction that the Lord sent with his blessings, but it was a hard conclusion to accept.

In 1643, the central pillar of Plymouth's religious vision died: William Brewster. Bradford's account of his death is the longest in his *Plimoth Plantation,* longer even than that of Squanto, and much longer, of course, than that of Dorothy. Brewster had reached eighty years — an age almost unheard of in his time, especially given the hardships he had faced. Bradford's memory of his death is one of the most touching in his writings:

> He had this blesing added by the Lord to all the rest, to die in his bed, in peace, amongst the midst of his freinds, who mourned and wepte over him, and ministered what help and comforte they could unto him, and he againe recomforted them whilst he could. His sicknes was not long, and till the last day therof he did not wholy keepe his bed. His speech continued till somewhat more then halfe a day, and then failed him; and about 9. or 10. a clock

that evning he died, without any pangs at all. A few hours before, he drew his breath shorte, and some few minutes before his last, he drew his breath long, as a man fallen into a sound slepe, without any pangs or gaspings, and so sweetly departed this life unto a better.

It was the end of an age, and Bradford sensed the changing wind. A few pages after he described Brewster's death, Bradford mused on God's hand on Plymouth, and the blessings he had given, "that notwithstanding the many changes and hardships that these people wente throwgh, and the many enemies they had and difficulties they mette with all, that so many of them should live to very olde age." If Plymouth town would not be a sign of God's providence and blessing, certainly this unnatural length of life was.

By the end of the 1640s, Bradford's discouragement was such that he would no longer continue his history of the colony, though he would live another decade. Brewster had gone now, most of the people had moved away, and even Edward Winslow, who had been such an aid to him in negotiating with the Indians, with the French and Dutch, with Massachusetts Bay, had gone back to England. Boston was burgeoning, with over fifteen thousand people, as little Plymouth shrank. And so Bradford put his manuscript away. Two centuries would pass before his words would be published. He did not know then that he had written a great account not only of the planting of a colony, but of God's loving and providential care of a people who had tried to carry out a vision that they had found in the Scriptures. Bradford thought he had failed in this vision; he did not understand how much he had succeeded.

CONCLUSION

"I Am Growne Aged"

Bradford's reputation as a fair, impartial man never faded among all the colonies of New England — not just Plymouth. But by the end of the 1640s, he had grown old under the burdens of his office; he was almost sixty — an old man by the standards of the times. In 1648, he was asked to negotiate a boundary dispute in New Haven between the Dutch and Massachusetts Bay. He asked to be excused because of "bodily infirmities" — the first time since the landing at Plymouth that there is any mention of any kind of physical weakness.

Bradford was still writing, but no longer history. He tried to impart his vision of God and obedience to a new generation, and so turned to poetry.

But keepe the truth in puriety
and walke in all humility
take heed of pride & contention

for that will bring distruction
Seeke love & peace & unity
and preserve faith, & sanctitie
and God will blesse you with his Grace
and bring you to his resting place.

Rest was much on his mind these days, but not rest as most think of it. He was reading in Latin and Greek. His own library was extensive — not as large as William Brewster's, but large enough to accommodate many volumes of religious and world history, including many works probably purchased from Brewster's estate.

He had also started to study Hebrew, and the reasons for this suggest much of Bradford: "Though I am growne aged, yet I have had a longing desire, to see with my owne eyes, something of that most ancient language, and holy tongue, in which the Law, and oracles of God were write; in which God, and angels spake to the holy patriarks, of old time; and what names were given to things, from the creation . . . for my owne contente."

Into the 1650s Bradford remained active, governing the colony, his own fields, his own trading. The general court of assistants continued to meet in his house, and the affairs of the colony centered around him. In 1655 he argued that he was too tired and old to continue as governor. There was, after all, a whole new generation of leaders — many of whom came from Bradford's own household. But he was elected anyway, and once more reluctantly agreed. The Pilgrims saw Bradford as the great patriarchal leader, the one who endured even as others fell away. Up in Boston, Winthrop died in 1649; Winslow died in 1655 at sea; and in Plymouth, Miles Standish died in 1656.

But throughout the next winter, Bradford was unwell. He had to miss the May court of 1657, only the second one he had ever

Bradford's grave on Burial Hill. On the headstone is carved, "Under this stone rest the ashes of William Bradford, a zealous Puritan and sincere Christian."

missed, and then on May 7, fell to his bed. That night, he dreamed warm dreams filled with images of a mother gathering her children unto her, just as God did. In the morning he told Alice that "God has given me a pledge of my happiness in another world." She would not believe the end was coming, but it was. He dictated his will that day, and died in the evening, "lamented," wrote Cotton Mather, "by all the Colonies of New England as a common Blessing and Father to them all."

Bradford would have been pleased to have been remembered as a father; he had never had one himself. And though he felt that he had failed in Plymouth, he had not. His was the first of the colonies to succeed in New England, and it provided the model for all the rest. The Pilgrim vision of church life would last to the present time and give rise to thousands and thousands of congregations that would choose their own ministers and their own way of worship. The principles by which he governed may be found demonstrated today during any New England spring, where the people of a township gather together to vote on how they shall be governed. The mutual roles of church and government that play themselves out in America today come not from the strong colony of Massachusetts Bay, but from Plymouth.

The vision of Plymouth survives because of William Bradford, a man of God who grabbed onto a continent and never let go.

Sources for This Book

No one can long work on a biography of William Bradford without journeying to Plymouth to stand on its shore. And it will not do to stop in at "Plimoth Plantation" on a sunny, bright June day, though that site certainly affords a sense of how the Pilgrims lived during their first years in the New World. But for the writer of a biography, it's best to go to Plymouth town in the winter, on one of the bitterly cold New England days when snow is in the air and the sea is gray and white. Standing on the shore and looking out to the long promontories that reach into the sea, you can almost imagine that your back is to a wilderness that stretches an unimaginable distance.

Turning around, you'll be thrust by the wind that scours the tops of the waves up toward Burial Hill, where you can wander among the whitened and lichened gravestones until you find the modest stone of William Bradford, and from there you can turn again and look down on the town that he founded, and beyond that, to the sea.

Toward the north you'll be able to make out the Pilgrim Hall Museum, and this book has been much influenced by the vision of the Pilgrim Fathers that the museum has so carefully and lovingly preserved. Though you will find no portrait of William Bradford there, for none exists, you will find his chair, and you may sit in a replica of it. Its knobby rigidity and straight, stern lines say something about the man. You'll also find, among the many exhibits, Miles Standish's sword, which says something about his height. My thanks and appreciation to Frances Leach and the Pilgrim Hall Museum for their kind and generous spirit in working with me and colleagues and students from Calvin College every January for lo, these last ten years. Their study, *An Adventure Almost Desperate* (Pilgrim Society, 1990), was an invaluable aid in my writing about the *Mayflower* and the journey to the New World. But in many ways, my biography is inspired by the work of this museum.

The first and greatest source about the Pilgrims, Plymouth, and William Bradford is Bradford's *Of Plimoth Plantation*. The first edition of this work was compiled by the Massachusetts Historical Society and published in 1856; you can still find it in old and rare bookshops, and it is worth holding the edition to have a sense of how it was first read by Americans. There are, of course, more modern editions of this work, the best of which is that of Samuel Eliot Morison (New York: Knopf, 1952, 1994). Most of the quotations from Bradford's work that are included in this biography are taken from my own copy of the first edition, though I have emended some of the spelling. Bradford and Winslow's earlier account of the colony, *Mourt's Relation,* is also an important source and available in a modern edition edited by Jordan D. Fiore (*Mourt's Relation: A Journal of the Pilgrims of Plymouth* [Plymouth: Plymouth Rock Foundation, 1985]).

There are scores and scores of books about the Pilgrims in general and William Bradford more specifically, but in this group are two that, though now older, still remain prominent and were crucial in my biography. Of these two, George F. Willison's *Saints and Strangers* (New York: Reynal & Hitchcock, 1945) is the best general study of the Pilgrim experience. Bradford Smith's *William Bradford* (Philadelphia: Lippincott, 1951) is the best biography of William Bradford himself. The best work which establishes the whole context for the Pilgrims and their voyage and puts them within the context of the founding of the New England colonies is another very old work, John Fiske's *The Beginnings of New England* (Boston: Houghton Mifflin, 1898), with illustrations and engravings that depict much of the world of the Pilgrims. And finally, a helpful book that focuses on the religious vision of the Pilgrims is Robert Bartlett's *The Faith of the Pilgrims* (New York: United Church Press, 1978).

Suggestions for Further Reading

Bradford, William. *Of Plymouth Plantation, 1620-1647.* Edited by Samuel Morison. New York: Knopf, 1994.

> Despite the difficulty of the language, this is a crucial source for understanding Bradford's own very strict perspective on the founding and meaning of Plymouth Colony. The spelling and punctuation have been modernized.

Burgess, Walter. *The Pastor of the Pilgrims.* New York: Harcourt, Brace, 1920.

> This biography of John Robinson deals with Robinson's Separatist beliefs and explores his influence on the Pilgrims — even when he was not among them.

Caffrey, Kate. *The Mayflower.* New York: Stein and Day, 1974.

An examination of the ship that brought the Pilgrims to the New World, telling the story of the Pilgrims by focusing on the boat. The book also explores the later history of the *Mayflower,* in both its physical and mythical senses.

Cline, Duane A. *Navigation in the Age of Discovery: An Introduction.* Rogers, Ark.: Montfleury, 1990.

For those interested in the voyages of the Pilgrims, this book provides insights into how the Pilgrims and their captains could make a landfall so precisely.

Daugherty, James. *The Landing of the Pilgrims.* New York: Random House, 1950.

Daugherty focuses specifically upon the *Mayflower* and the early years of the colony. The book is illustrated with Daugherty's typically heroic and muscular artistic renderings of scenes.

Dexter, Henry M., and Morgan Dexter. *The England and Holland of the Pilgrims.* 1906. Reprint, Baltimore: Genealogical Publishing Co., 1978.

This work deals principally with the early lives of the Separatists while they were living in Amsterdam and Leyden.

Harris, John. *Saga of the Pilgrims: From Europe to the New World.* Chester, Conn.: Globe Pequot Press, 1990.

An engaging and readable narrative of the journey of the Pilgrims to Plymouth. This book does not specifically focus on Bradford alone, but examines all of the Pilgrim experience well.

James, Sydney V., ed. *Three Visitors to Early Plymouth*. Plymouth: Plimoth Plantation, 1963.

A collection of contemporary letters by Emmanuel Altham, John Pory, and Isaac de Rasieres describing Plymouth Colony in its earliest years.

Langdon, George D., Jr. *Pilgrim Colony: A History of New Plymouth, 1620-1691*. New Haven: Yale University Press, 1966.

One of the best-written general histories of Plymouth Colony's inception and development through the seventeenth century.

Leynse, James P. *Preceding the Mayflower*. New York: Fountainhead Books, 1972.

This book examines the lives of the Pilgrims in England and in the Netherlands, concluding with the voyage of the *Mayflower*.

Mather, Cotton. *Magnalia Christi Americana*. 1852. Reprint, New York: Russell & Russell, 1967.

Cotton Mather recounts the story of Bradford's life in this longer work; it is the primary source for the details of Bradford's early life, as well as the scene at his deathbed.

Stratton, Eugene A. *Plymouth Colony: Its History and People: 1620-1691*. Salt Lake City: Ancestry Publications, 1986.

This work examines the history of Plymouth up until the time the colony was finally absorbed by the Massachusetts Bay Colony, some three decades after Bradford's death. While it, too, narrates the larger story of the Pilgrims, it is particularly useful for the biographical information it gives about Pilgrims other than Bradford.

Wilbur, C. Keith. *The New England Indians.* Chester, Conn.: Globe Pequot Press, 1990.

This is an important source for understanding the nature of the several tribes who met the Pilgrims, and gives insights about their relationships with Plymouth and their suspicions about the colony.

Young, Alexander, ed. *Chronicles of the Pilgrim Fathers.* 1844. Reprint, Baltimore: Genealogical Publishing Co., 1974. Reprinted as Edward Winslow, *Good News from New England.* Bedford, Mass.: Applewood Books, 1996.

This edition of Edward Winslow's *Good News from New England,* written in 1624, chronicles the activities of Plymouth Colony during the years 1622 and 1623.

Photo Credits

The publisher wishes to gratefully acknowledge the following archives and individuals for permission to use their images as interior illustrations.

The images on pages 10, 13, 58, 89, 93, 130 are courtesy of the Library of Congress.

The images on pages 66, 76, 83, 135 are courtesy North Wind Picture Archives.

The images on pages 115, 160 are courtesy of the Bettman Archive.

The images on the fronticepiece, and pages 108, 171, and 179 are courtesy of the Pilgrim Society, Plymouth, Massachusetts.

The images on pages 61, 84, 85, 96, 104, 116, 124, 125, 127, 143, 145, 147, 150, 156, 157 are courtesy of the Plimouth Plantation, Plymouth, Massachusetts.

The image on page 168 is courtesy of the State Library of Massachusetts.

The images on pages 48, and 107 are courtesy of the Mary Evans Picture Library.

The photograph on page 3 is taken by Nicholas Servian FIIP, courtesy of Woodmansterne Limited.

The photographs on pages 35, and 185 are courtesy of Crispin Gill.

The painting on page 53 entitled, The Departure of the Pilgrim Fathers, by B. F. Gribble, is courtesy of Dr. L.H. Hurrell.

The images on pages 5, 15, 22, 32, 45, 49, 50, 56, 71, 120, 164, 175 are courtesy of Gayle Brown.

While every effort has been made to trace and contact copyright holders, this has not always been possible. If contacted, the publisher will be pleased to correct any errors or omissions at the earliest opportunity.

Index